I WONDER

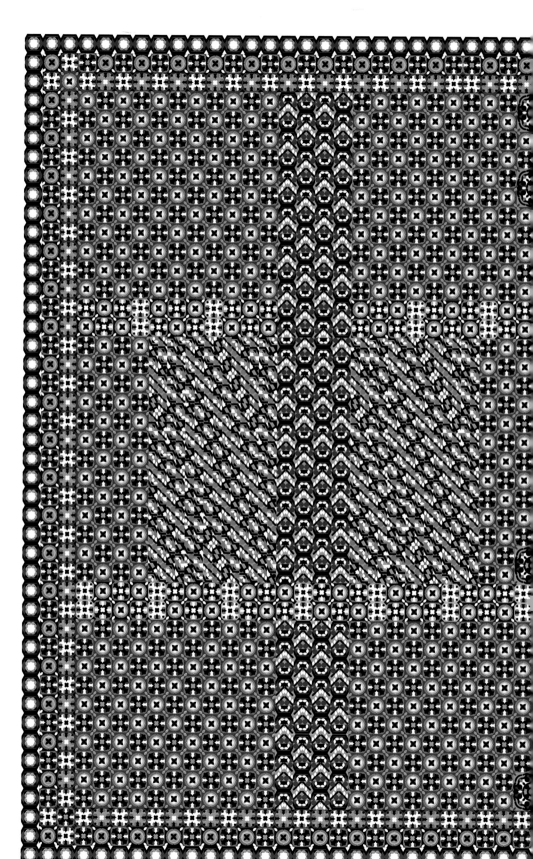

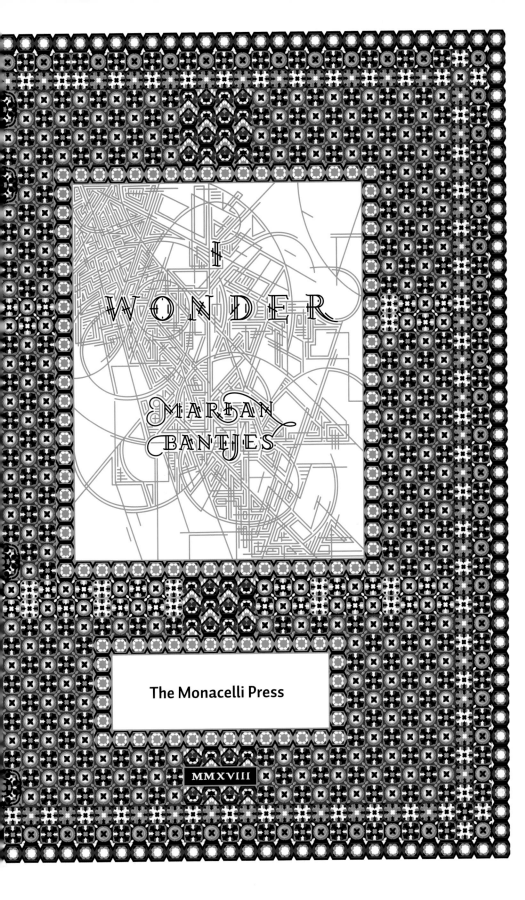

I
WONDER

MARIAN
BANTJES

The Monacelli Press

MMXVIII

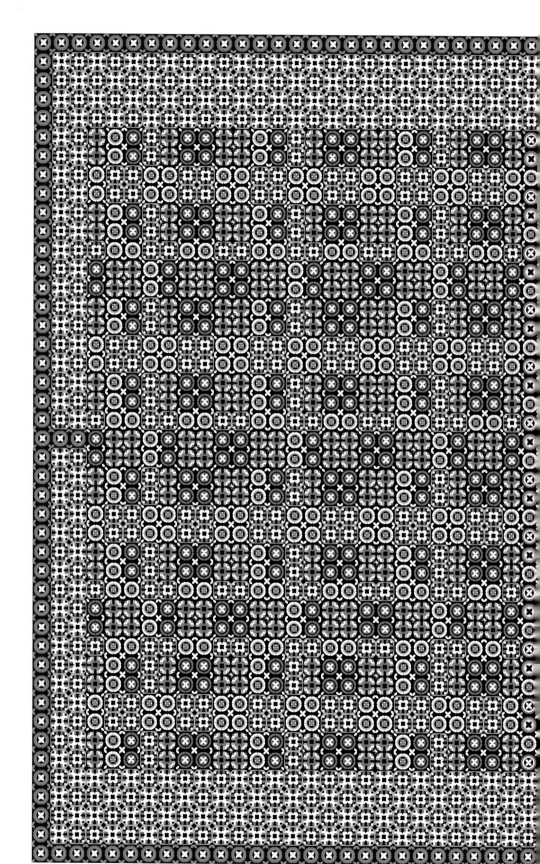

Dedicated to my mother
June Bantjes,
who always encouraged me
to make my own.

I wish you were here.

I Wonder © 2010, 2018 Marian Bantjes

First published in 2010 in the United States
by The Monacelli Press. This new and expanded
edition 2018.

Library of Congress Control Number: 2018939266
ISBN 978-1-58093-519-7
10 9 8 7 6 5 4 3 2 1

Second American Edition

Printed in China

Design by Marian Bantjes

The Monacelli Press
6 West 18th Street
New York, New York 10011
www.monacellipress.com

CONTENTS

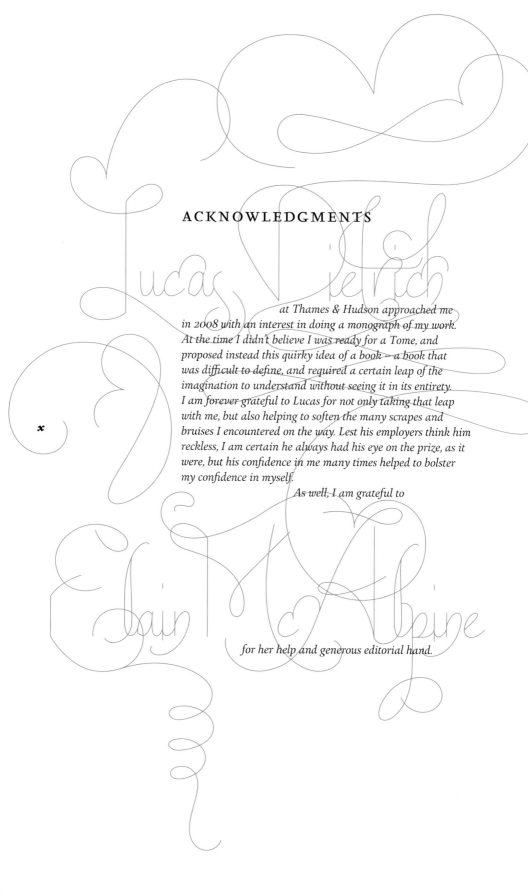

ACKNOWLEDGMENTS

at Thames & Hudson approached me in 2008 with an interest in doing a monograph of my work. At the time I didn't believe I was ready for a Tome, and proposed instead this quirky idea of a book – a book that was difficult to define, and required a certain leap of the imagination to understand without seeing it in its entirety. I am forever grateful to Lucas for not only taking that leap with me, but also helping to soften the many scrapes and bruises I encountered on the way. Lest his employers think him reckless, I am certain he always had his eye on the prize, as it were, but his confidence in me many times helped to bolster my confidence in myself.

As well, I am grateful to

for her help and generous editorial hand.

If I thanked everyone in my life who has supported me in my work and my career, this list would be very long, and never complete. So I'll stick to acknowledging those who helped me directly with this book, while assuring the rest that I remember them and am grateful for everything they've done that got me to this point.

Early in the process of writing, I found myself lost in a maze of research and fascinating but long-winded asides, and if it were not for my brother

I might never have found my way out. His ability to not only critique my writing, but to cut to the heart of what I was trying to say while knowing exactly who I am and the voice I write in, both astounded and elated me. He set me straight, or as straight as can be.

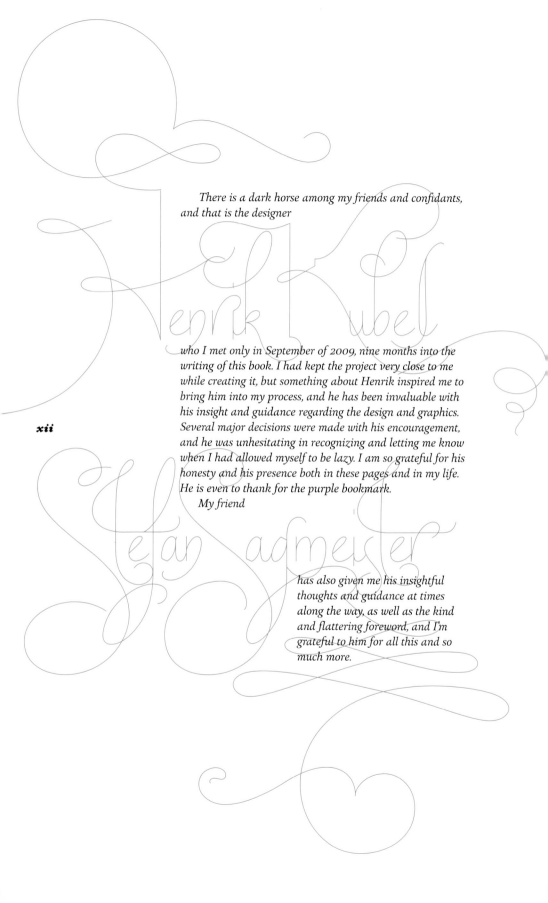

There is a dark horse among my friends and confidants, and that is the designer *Henrik Kubel* who I met only in September of 2009, nine months into the writing of this book. I had kept the project very close to me while creating it, but something about Henrik inspired me to bring him into my process, and he has been invaluable with his insight and guidance regarding the design and graphics. Several major decisions were made with his encouragement, and he was unhesitating in recognizing and letting me know when I had allowed myself to be lazy. I am so grateful for his honesty and his presence both in these pages and in my life. He is even to thank for the purple bookmark.

My friend *Stefan Sagmeister* has also given me his insightful thoughts and guidance at times along the way, as well as the kind and flattering foreword, and I'm grateful to him for all this and so much more.

xii

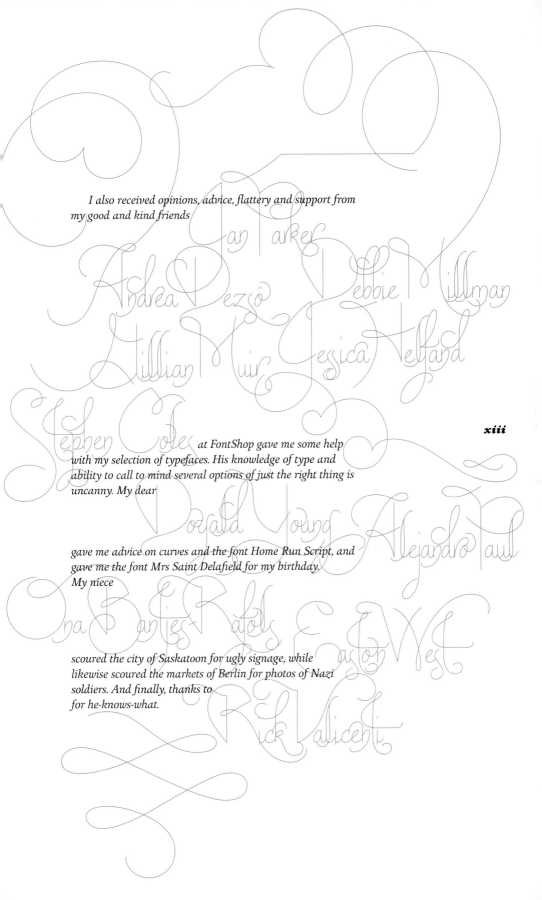

I also received opinions, advice, flattery and support from my good and kind friends

Jan Parker

Andrea Dezsö   Debbie Millman

Lillian Muir   Jessica Helfand

Stephen Coles *at FontShop gave me some help with my selection of typefaces. His knowledge of type and ability to call to mind several options of just the right thing is uncanny. My dear*

Donald Young   Alejandro Paul

gave me advice on curves and the font Home Run Script, and gave me the font Mrs Saint Delafield for my birthday. My niece

Ona Banties Katols E EWest   Easton West

scoured the city of Saskatoon for ugly signage, while likewise scoured the markets of Berlin for photos of Nazi soldiers. And finally, thanks to for he-knows-what.

Rick Valicenti

Spring

by Stefan Sagmeister

arian is beautiful.

And her typographic pinnacles are gorgeous. It is their beauty that makes me read them; it is their beauty that makes me consider their meaning; it is their beauty that makes me keep at them, even if they occasionally resist easy decipherment.

Marian's work might be my favourite example of beauty facilitating the communication of meaning.

And ... she never lets me down. The expectations raised by her immaculate form are matched by the significance of the content. Ultimately it's not how she says it, but what she has to say. It's like meeting a supermodel who turns out to be a neuroscientist.

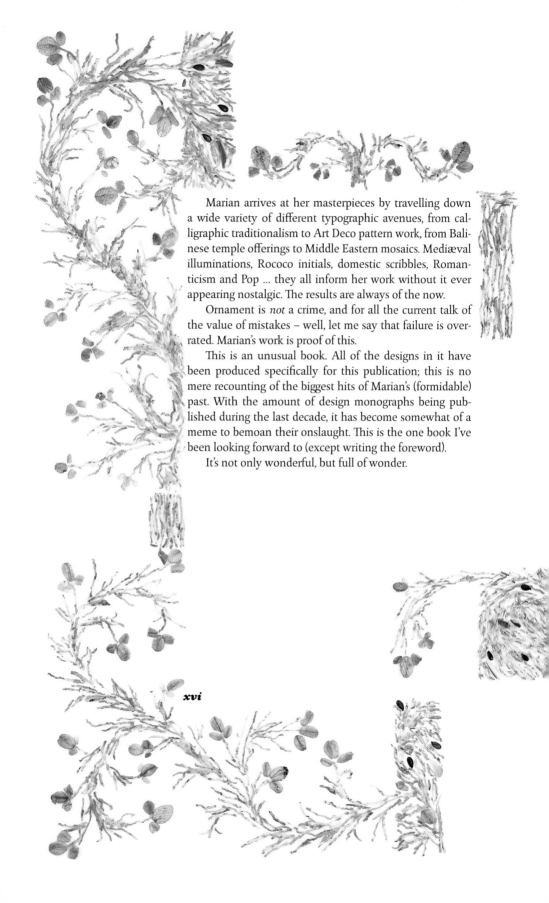

Marian arrives at her masterpieces by travelling down a wide variety of different typographic avenues, from calligraphic traditionalism to Art Deco pattern work, from Balinese temple offerings to Middle Eastern mosaics. Mediæval illuminations, Rococo initials, domestic scribbles, Romanticism and Pop ... they all inform her work without it ever appearing nostalgic. The results are always of the now.

Ornament is *not* a crime, and for all the current talk of the value of mistakes – well, let me say that failure is overrated. Marian's work is proof of this.

This is an unusual book. All of the designs in it have been produced specifically for this publication; this is no mere recounting of the biggest hits of Marian's (formidable) past. With the amount of design monographs being published during the last decade, it has become somewhat of a meme to bemoan their onslaught. This is the one book I've been looking forward to (except writing the foreword).

It's not only wonderful, but full of wonder.

xvi

'*For we are not sent into this world to do any thing into which we cannot put our hearts.*'

JOHN RUSKIN,
THE SEVEN LAMPS OF ARCHITECTURE,
1849

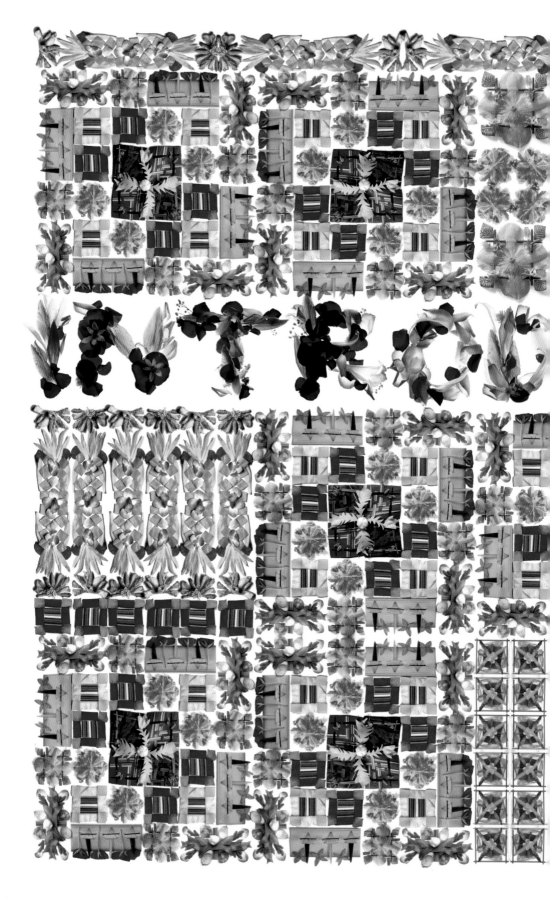

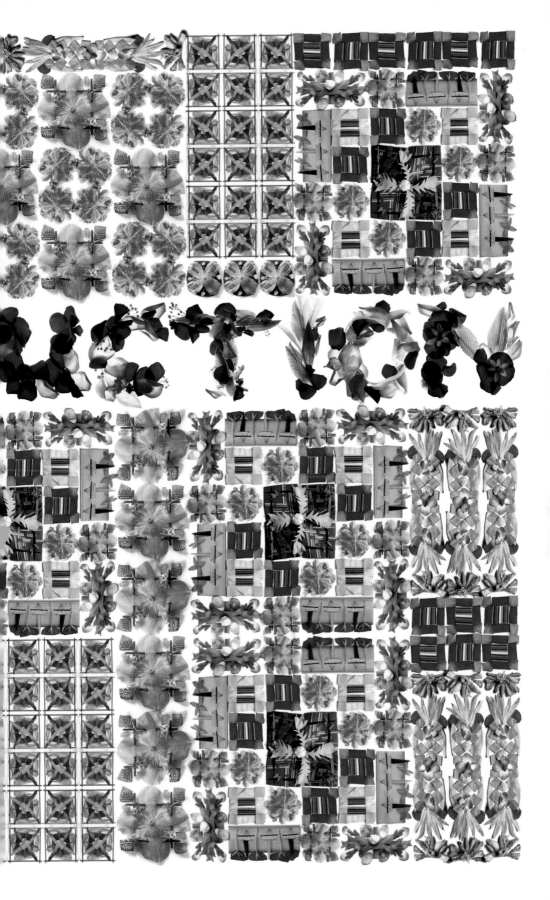

hen I began this book, I imagined it as a collection of essays, some of which I had already written for the web, and some of which I would write from scratch, to follow ideas I had been contemplating on the themes of wonder, honour and memory. My first surprise came when I set about what I had intended to be a light edit of the articles I'd already published on the web. While I'd considered them nearly finished, I realized that when I imagined them *in print*, they were not nearly ready. Further, as I rolled up my sleeves to get them into shape and began the research required to do so, I was horrified to discover how frankly incorrect some of them were. The inaccuracies contained in the web version of 'Ye Olde Graphic Designer' alone were enough to make me disavow authorship. What I gained in veracity, however, I lost in a certain irreverent immediacy of writing style. The barbed, humorous tone – complete with taunts and jibes – of my original versions was somehow lost, despite my best intentions. There's no doubt in my mind that the web and the printed page are two different places that afford different styles in writing and presentation. The web versions supposed an almost tangible audience, which would respond directly and quickly to my virtual self. The versions

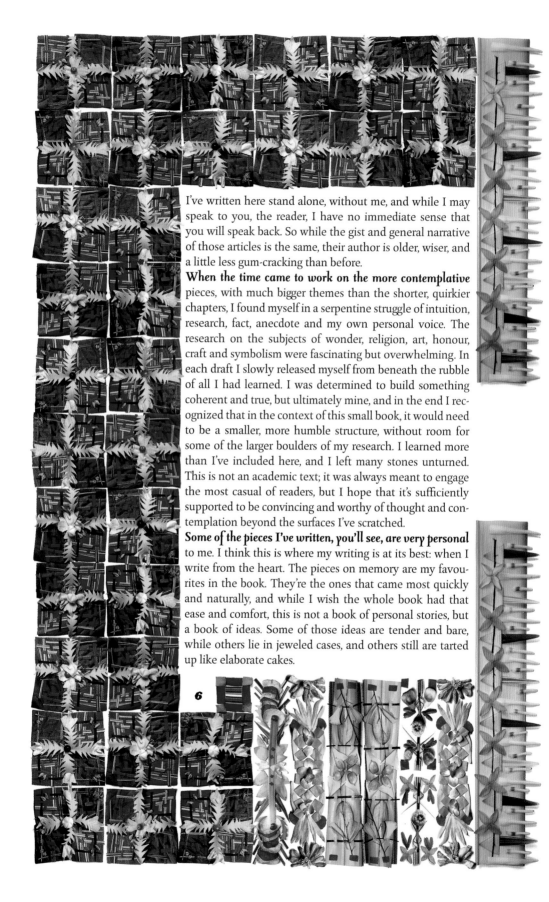

I've written here stand alone, without me, and while I may speak to you, the reader, I have no immediate sense that you will speak back. So while the gist and general narrative of those articles is the same, their author is older, wiser, and a little less gum-cracking than before.

When the time came to work on the more contemplative pieces, with much bigger themes than the shorter, quirkier chapters, I found myself in a serpentine struggle of intuition, research, fact, anecdote and my own personal voice. The research on the subjects of wonder, religion, art, honour, craft and symbolism were fascinating but overwhelming. In each draft I slowly released myself from beneath the rubble of all I had learned. I was determined to build something coherent and true, but ultimately mine, and in the end I recognized that in the context of this small book, it would need to be a smaller, more humble structure, without room for some of the larger boulders of my research. I learned more than I've included here, and I left many stones unturned. This is not an academic text; it was always meant to engage the most casual of readers, but I hope that it's sufficiently supported to be convincing and worthy of thought and contemplation beyond the surfaces I've scratched.

Some of the pieces I've written, you'll see, are very personal to me. I think this is where my writing is at its best: when I write from the heart. The pieces on memory are my favourites in the book. They're the ones that came most quickly and naturally, and while I wish the whole book had that ease and comfort, this is not a book of personal stories, but a book of ideas. Some of those ideas are tender and bare, while others lie in jeweled cases, and others still are tarted up like elaborate cakes.

I was never worried about the varied tone and eclecticism of these pieces; it was, in fact, their seeming disparity that was part of my original vision for the book. But in writing it, I've been amazed how this disparity has merged into a surprising cohesiveness throughout the course of the book. There are definite themes and threads that turn up in unexpected places. In writing and rereading, I've had many an *aha!* moment, with no small amount of self-satisfied pleasure from my own unintended cleverness. So while there's no particular reason you shouldn't read the book in pieces, while skipping about, I suspect that there is something more to be gained by reading it through from front to back.

As if my struggles with the writing weren't enough, there is also, quite obviously, another dimension to the book in the graphics and design. My intention was always to illustrate without illustrating; to avoid the *figure a* form of illustration. Not that I have anything against figure a, but as an idea among a book of ideas, I want to show that there are different ways to treat visuals, and that it's possible to make a fully integrated document where the words and images are interdependent, neither able to fully survive without the other. The text is not the same without the imagery, the imagery is not the same without the text. This brings me back to the web, and my intent to make something that is necessarily a book, and which could not be as rich of an experience on the web as it is in your hands ... certainly not now, in the early part of the second decade of the 21st century. I'm fairly certain that there will come a time, probably in the not-too-distant future, when a digital version of this book in some form will be all that print could ever make it, and perhaps more. But for now, it has been specifically

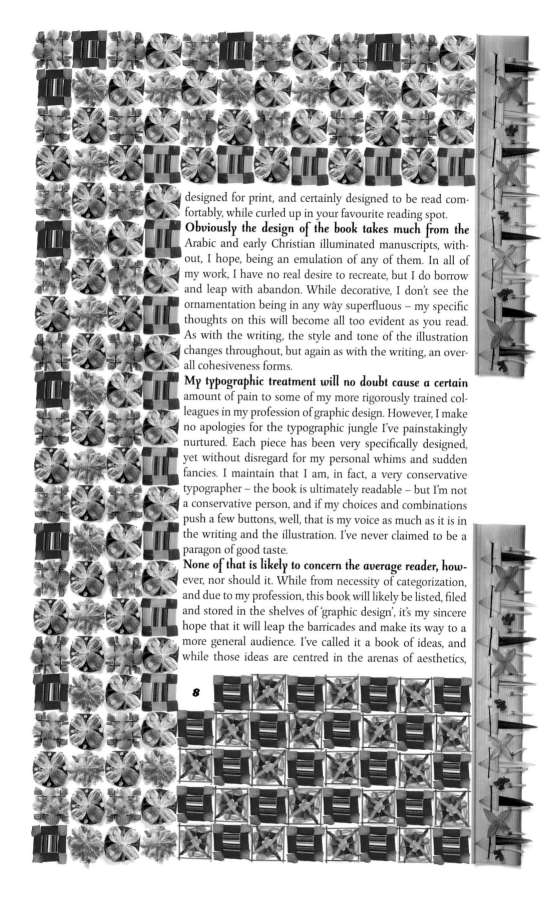

designed for print, and certainly designed to be read comfortably, while curled up in your favourite reading spot.

Obviously the design of the book takes much from the Arabic and early Christian illuminated manuscripts, without, I hope, being an emulation of any of them. In all of my work, I have no real desire to recreate, but I do borrow and leap with abandon. While decorative, I don't see the ornamentation being in any way superfluous – my specific thoughts on this will become all too evident as you read. As with the writing, the style and tone of the illustration changes throughout, but again as with the writing, an overall cohesiveness forms.

My typographic treatment will no doubt cause a certain amount of pain to some of my more rigorously trained colleagues in my profession of graphic design. However, I make no apologies for the typographic jungle I've painstakingly nurtured. Each piece has been very specifically designed, yet without disregard for my personal whims and sudden fancies. I maintain that I am, in fact, a very conservative typographer – the book is ultimately readable – but I'm not a conservative person, and if my choices and combinations push a few buttons, well, that is my voice as much as it is in the writing and the illustration. I've never claimed to be a paragon of good taste.

None of that is likely to concern the average reader, how-ever, nor should it. While from necessity of categorization, and due to my profession, this book will likely be listed, filed and stored in the shelves of 'graphic design', it's my sincere hope that it will leap the barricades and make its way to a more general audience. I've called it a book of ideas, and while those ideas are centred in the arenas of aesthetics,

8

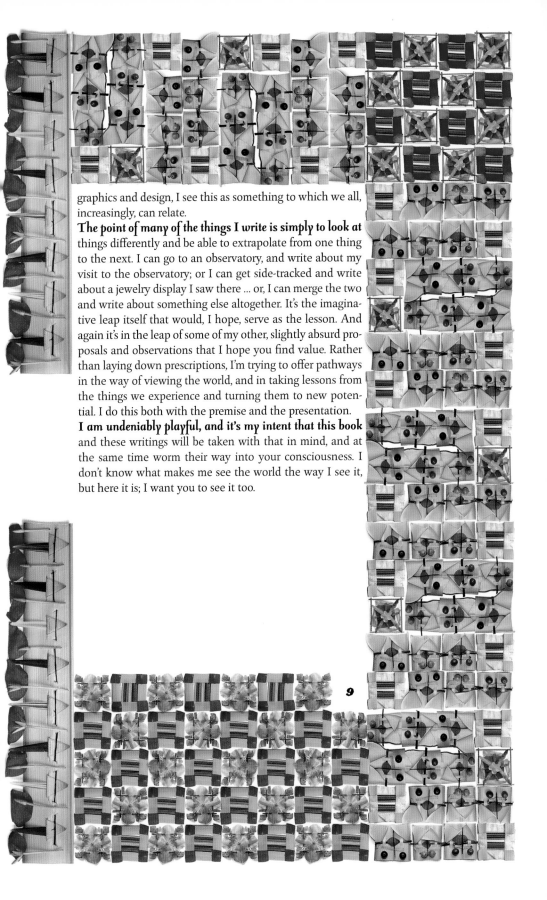

graphics and design, I see this as something to which we all, increasingly, can relate.

The point of many of the things I write is simply to look at things differently and be able to extrapolate from one thing to the next. I can go to an observatory, and write about my visit to the observatory; or I can get side-tracked and write about a jewelry display I saw there ... or, I can merge the two and write about something else altogether. It's the imaginative leap itself that would, I hope, serve as the lesson. And again it's in the leap of some of my other, slightly absurd proposals and observations that I hope you find value. Rather than laying down prescriptions, I'm trying to offer pathways in the way of viewing the world, and in taking lessons from the things we experience and turning them to new potential. I do this both with the premise and the presentation.

I am undeniably playful, and it's my intent that this book and these writings will be taken with that in mind, and at the same time worm their way into your consciousness. I don't know what makes me see the world the way I see it, but here it is; I want you to see it too.

9

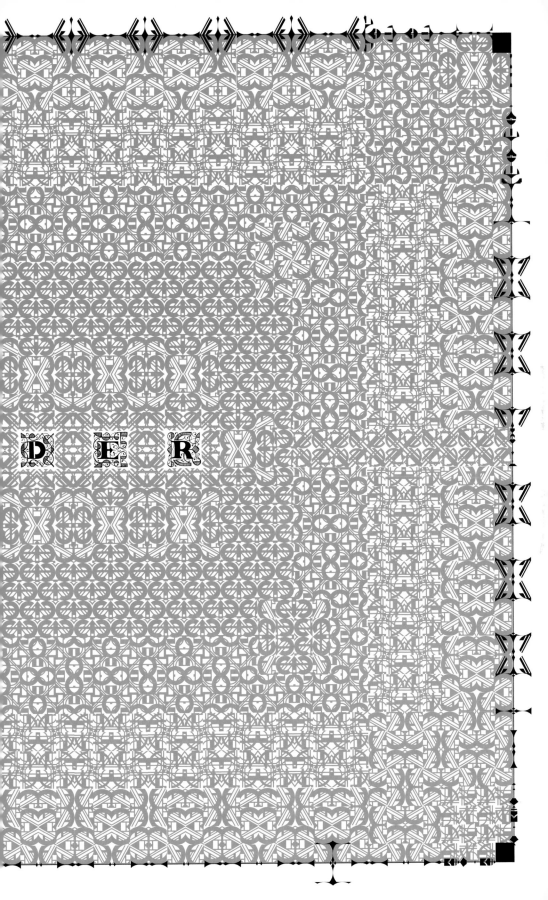

D E R

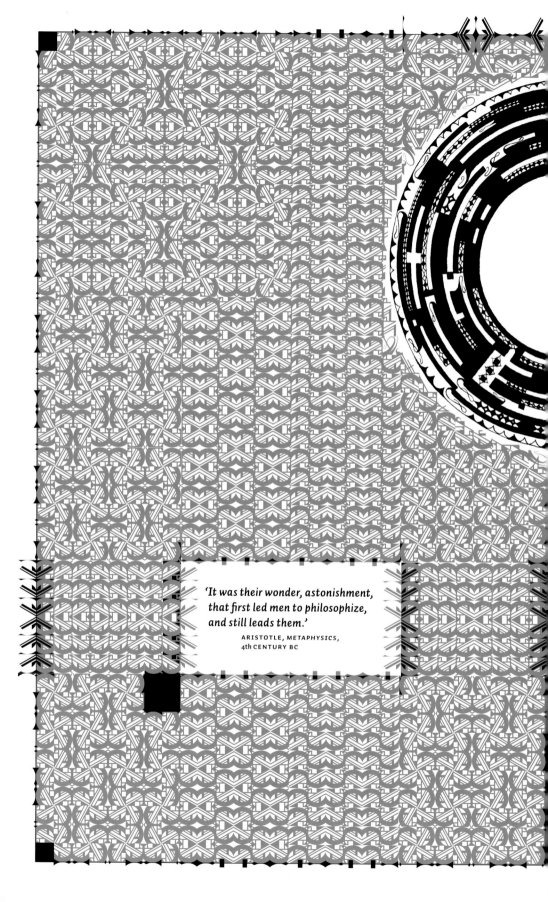

'It was their wonder, astonishment,
that first led men to philosophize,
and still leads them.'

ARISTOTLE, METAPHYSICS,
4th CENTURY BC

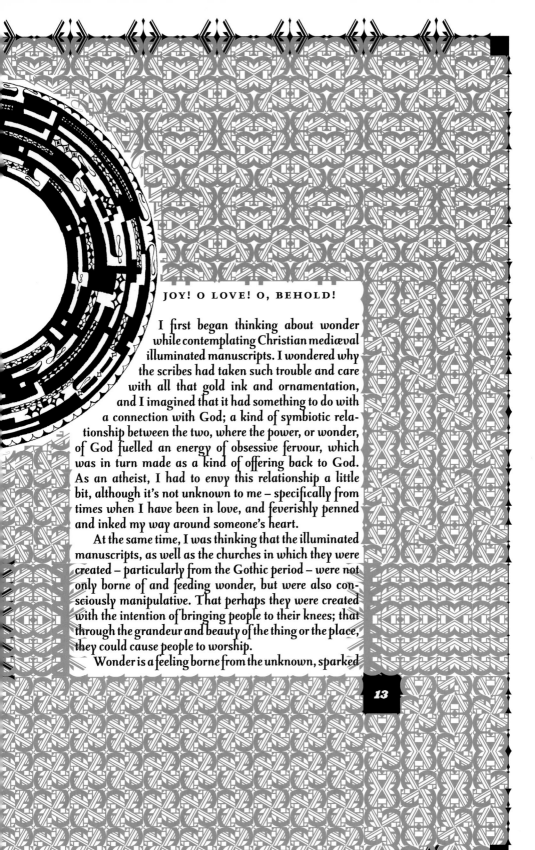

JOY! O LOVE! O, BEHOLD!

I first began thinking about wonder while contemplating Christian mediæval illuminated manuscripts. I wondered why the scribes had taken such trouble and care with all that gold ink and ornamentation, and I imagined that it had something to do with a connection with God; a kind of symbiotic relationship between the two, where the power, or wonder, of God fuelled an energy of obsessive fervour, which was in turn made as a kind of offering back to God. As an atheist, I had to envy this relationship a little bit, although it's not unknown to me – specifically from times when I have been in love, and feverishly penned and inked my way around someone's heart.

At the same time, I was thinking that the illuminated manuscripts, as well as the churches in which they were created – particularly from the Gothic period – were not only borne of and feeding wonder, but were also consciously manipulative. That perhaps they were created with the intention of bringing people to their knees; that through the grandeur and beauty of the thing or the place, they could cause people to worship.

Wonder is a feeling borne from the unknown, sparked

by the desire for enlightenment. It contains elation, joy, and sometimes a hint of fear, but it's a deeply pleasurable and sometimes spiritual emotion. Deeper than astonishment, delight or amazement, it's related to awe, which is reverential to a higher power, and to curiosity, which is what killed the cat. It's the feeling that something is just beyond our grasp, combined with enough knowledge to make the mind seek. It exists in the gap between the truly incomprehensible (which is precluded by defeat), and the comprehensible (which is taken for granted). Although we understand the nature of flowers and the existence of stars and planets, we're still able to stop in that moment of not understanding how something so beautiful or so vast or so complex could possibly exist. We experience this in life, love, science, religion and art.

Wonder in nature is what led us to the wonders of science, but for centuries, the wonder of art has been just as powerful. People have been working images into materials for all of recorded history. Our ability to transform one thing into another is one of our great gifts, and our ability to do so with virtuosity is a cause for wonderment. Artists themselves were often compelled to believe that they weren't responsible for what they made, but that some divine force worked through them. Sometimes that direction is from above, from a god or spirit, through the artist to his hands, and other times it's in the opposite direction, as a kind of transcendence from the art through the body to the god.

When we look at great works of art, we feel this power. We may be awed by the artist's skill, or by luminescence (as in a painting by Vermeer), by balance and perfection, by an abundance of detail, a wealth of materials or incredible craft. Whatever it is that captures us in this way, there is a feeling of something that is not ourselves.

'The walls of these buildings were not cold and forbidding. They were formed of stained glass that shone like rubies and emeralds. Everything that was heavenly, earthly or humdrum was eliminated. The faithful who surrendered themselves to the contemplation of all this beauty could feel that they had come nearer to understanding the mysteries of a realm beyond the reach of matter.'

E.H. GOMBRICH,
THE STORY OF ART (London, 1950; 2006), 142.

WONDERS

In historian Lorraine Daston's book *Wonders and the Order of Nature, 1150–1750*, she discusses the wonders of earlier centuries: monsters, science and the contents of Wunderkammern – cabinets of curiosities filled with strange artifacts, including mysterious objects from the natural world: unicorns' horns, gryphon claws and eggs, and preserved deformities in humans, animals and vegetables. These things were valued because they were unknown, or relics from the unknown, brought to Europe by travellers from other parts of the globe. They alluded to the world of magic and the supernatural, and were often thought to have magical powers. Man-made things, too, accompanied and enhanced these articles from nature. Corals and nautilus shells were embellished with gold, made into urns and chalices, or used as materials in whimsical scenes and other items, making them even more astonishing in their appearance through transformation. Gems were valued for

15

their beauty and rarity, but were also thought to have supernatural properties, each associated with different virtues. Combined with beautifully worked precious metals, these qualities were enhanced, signifying not only great wealth, but power – power over people, over nature, and magic.[1]

Transformation from art to nature and nature to art was a common theme. Stones such as marble and agate, which seemed to spontaneously contain scenes and other images, joined the art of the virtuoso – the craftsman who could turn ivory into lace, or pearls into tiny body parts. In an extreme example from the seventeenth century, Dutch anatomist Frederik Ruysch created dioramas with infant human skeletons arranged in landscapes where preserved bladders and kidney stones posed as rocks, and bronchial tubes stood for trees![2]

Noblemen displayed the treasures of their Wunderkammern, including living animals, dwarves, giants and a panoply of exoticism, using the power of wonder to enhance their status. But I was surprised to discover that churches also held great collections, and, in a bizarre marriage of religion and sideshow, used them to draw people in to prompt this spark of emotional wonder. This was one of my *aha!* moments. It seems I wasn't so cynical after all in thinking the embellishment of religious artifacts may be manipulative in intent, for there were a number of cases where the mirabilia of ostrich eggs, whale ribs or meteorites were used to lure people inside the church – even, in one hilarious depiction, a stuffed

> '*From the wonders of Nature is the nearest passage to the wonders of Art.*'
>
> FRANCIS BACON,
> THE ADVANCEMENT OF LEARNING,
> 1605

1 Lorraine Daston and Katharine Park, *Wonders and the Order of Nature*, 1150–1750 (New York, 1998), 67, 69, 76, 266.

2 James Trilling, *Ornament: A Modern Perspective* (Seattle, 2003), 161.

3 Daston and Park, 86, 101, 107.

crocodile permanently mounted, dangling from the ceiling.[3] Rationalized as proof of the greatness of God, maybe, but still. In this, wonders fell from the heavens and shared the cabinet with curiosities: magic slumming with two-headed calves; angels with Bat-boy.

Over time, Wunderkammern fell from favour, as collectors outdid each other with increasingly huge and eclectic displays. Travellers of the time became weary with the endlessly repetitive compilations of curiosities. When you've seen one unicorn horn, you've seen them all. What was wondrous became mundane. Astonishment over plenitude replaced the wonder of the particular; much as a hurried visit to the Louvre today can invoke blasé fatigue, people became overwhelmed and underwhelmed at the same time.

BEAUTY

Outside of the wonder of exoticism, there prevailed a wonder of beauty. For centuries, ornament has served as a pathway to the divine. We are captivated by the repetitions and transformations of pattern, drawn in to the minutiae of detail, intrigued by beautiful and complex forms, and seduced by precious metals, stones, gems and other materials. It was in the Middle Ages that art reached its apotheosis as a Christian vehicle for wonder with its ability to uplift and transform. The vaulted ceilings of the Gothic cathedrals became ever greater in

'When out of my delight in the beauty of the house of God the loveliness of the many-coloured stones has called me away from external cares, and worthy meditation has induced me to reflect, transferring that which is material to that which is immaterial...'

ABBOT SUGER OF ST DENIS, LIBER DE REBUS IN ADMINISTRATIONE SUA GESTIS, 1144–48

17

height, held up by impossible delicacy and containing large openings for brilliantly coloured stained-glass windows.

The Christian illuminated manuscripts contain an interesting mix of these wonders of beauty, combined with peculiar sideshow antics of their own. Images of devotion share space with drolleries, where figures impishly loiter about the margins. With animals and other creatures of whimsy, they serve as a kind of Wunderkammer of the page – one is reminded of the minor characters of Shakespeare, who support the main theme with bumbling, raucous commentary. It is here, too, that elements of magic and superstition lie. Doors, windows and the covers of books were thought to be foci for supernatural attack, so these were particularly embellished, often with knotwork, which was believed to have protective power by confusing evil spirits, who would become lost in the maze of complex designs.[4] One man's wonder is another's confusion. These intricate artworks are not only visually wondrous, but amaze us with their investment of time, skill and infinite detail.

Again, however, the purpose of some of these illuminations is revealed as a persuasive tactic. The beautiful pages, illustrated with images of Christ, served missionaries as objects of wonder in aid of persuasion. By holding the books open, facing the viewer, they were more readily able to attract the desired attention from those they sought to convert.

> 'It was evidently very important that right from the outset the monks should exhibit a visual image of the new religion which could be seen and wondered over even before they began explaining the message of the Scripture.'
>
> CHRISTOPHER DE HAMEL,
> *A HISTORY OF ILLUMINATED MANUSCRIPTS* (London, 2006), 14.

THE POLITICS
OF WONDER & ORNAMENT

The history of wonder contains some surprising controversies: Aristotle valued it as the impetus to inquiry, but in early Christianity, to seek knowledge was not necessarily a virtue. The unquestioning wonder of God was acceptable, but curiosity was considered a vice. A debate over 'seemly wonder' and what kind of inquiry was acceptable to the Church raged on for centuries, touching on 'the fearful wonder of the vulgar', 'the pleasurable wonder that informed' and 'the wonder of the connoisseur', as philosophers rejected and accepted it in varying degrees.[5]

I felt a strong connection from these debates over the seemliness of wonder to the philosophical and aesthetic debates over ornament, which also flared up over the centuries, and the complaints against both are not dissimilar.

In Europe, ornamentation became increasingly associated with deceit. Virtuosity began to be seen as artifice by placing the appearance of perfection over the reality of intrinsic beauty. That which was meant to honour God began to compete. There was a view that the wonder of man-made things took the viewer away from, rather than to, God. Ornamentation dazzled too much and led to temptation and idolatry. With the advent of Protestantism in the sixteenth century, there

'…so strong is the popular sense of the unworthiness and insignificance of things purely emotional … These philosophers seem to feel that unless moral and aesthetic judgements are the expression of objective truth, and not merely expressions of human nature, they stand condemned of hopeless triviality.'

GEORGE SANTAYANA,
THE SENSE OF BEAUTY: BEING THE
OUTLINE OF AESTHETIC THEORY
(New York, 1985), 4–5.

4   Trilling, *The Language of Ornament*, 135.
5   Daston and Park, 123–124, 167.

was a movement to remove any distraction from a direct relation to God. The discourse around ornament and embellishment became a moral one: what once elevated was viewed with suspicion and resentment towards the expense of wasteful indulgences, and became synonymous with artifice and sensuality.

The politics surrounding ornamentation are ancient. Both Socrates and, later, Cicero inveighed against flourishes in speech on the grounds that it seduced while obscuring the truth. Vitruvius objected to Roman ornamentation that defied the laws of nature. Hybrid animals, figures resting on obviously insubstantial supports or sprouting from leaves (a cry taken up again in 1754 by Charles-Nicolas Cochin, in response to the overly florid forms of Rococo)[6] – these motifs were seen as 'monsters' of ornamentation, not unlike the inhabitants of the Wunderkammern, where fish shared bodies with humans and horses sprouted wings and horns.

In the nineteenth century, Augustus Pugin decried the use of faux dimensionality on walls and floors, and others saw ornament as the 'embodiment of morbid sexuality and the dangerously seductive powers of fantasy'.[7] Ornament's ability to inspire wonder and the imagination became a doorway to temptation, the perversion of nature and dangerous illusion. Where the transformation of the spirit was desirable, the transformation of reality was not.

'Rococo dealt Western visual culture a blow even neoclassicism could not heal. By threatening to dissolve reality itself, rococo ornament fed the deep-seated fears of excess, artifice and transformation, and focused them on a single target.'

TRILLING, ORNAMENT: A MODERN PERSPECTIVE, 160.

20

6   E.H. Gombrich, *The Sense of Order: A Study in the Psychology of Decorative Art* (London, 1979; 1984), 18–21, 34.
7   Trilling, *Ornament: A Modern Perspective*, 117.
8   Gombrich, *The Sense of Order*, 48–49.

Even the transformation of materials, once found astonishing, was now seen as dishonest. While I feel there is a difference between carving wood so that it appears like wrought iron, and discovering that what looks like carved stone is instead formed plaster, that difference seems to have been all but nullified by the villainy of deceit. Among the many 'rules' of ornament and craft that ebbed and flowed from the eighteenth to the twentieth century was the call for materials to respect their natural properties; glass should be made to look like glass, for example, and no other. Whether this was in the ostensible respect for nature or an elitist attempt to keep articles and their owners from appearing as something more elevated than they really were, the result was one step further away from imagination in the direction of rationalism.

In the mid-nineteenth century, Gottfried Semper summed up all of these arguments when he said, 'Art should apply the laws of nature rather than imitate nature … paying proper regard to the relation of purpose, material and technique.'[8]

Ornament was under attack, and the prevailing sense, even among those who fought against modernity, such as John Ruskin and William Morris in the late nineteenth century, was that ornament needed to operate within certain bounds, for the sake of propriety, honesty and matters of taste. No more fantastical whimsy, no expensive bejewelment, no play in the realms of the imagination. Ruskin even went so far as to deny virtuosity, feeling that fine work was an 'inheritance of ignorance and cruelty', and that to work something to a fine finish was the work of slavery.[9] Ultimately, after all the rules had sifted out, one type of ornament was still allowed: that which was 'indeterminate'. The natural beauty of materials was allowed to stand for itself, and it is with some irony that we note the return of marble and layered stone (in the architecture of Adolf Loos), that old relic from the Wunderkammer, with its mysterious designs formed by nature.

THE MODERN WORLD

The path from here to twentieth-century Modernism is short. As the battle over ornament raged on into the late nineteenth century, new technologies further threatened the wonders of art and craft. In textiles, for instance, the most valued cloths were made with the finest weaving, where regularity and perfection inspired awe in the skill of the maker. But with the advent of mechanical looms, perfection became the everyday, and these potentially wondrous machines quickly grew into some not-so-wonderful factories. Machinery for the production of other artifacts was also on the rise, but instead of producing perfection, they produced mass quantities of poor imitations.

The market was flooded with cheap goods in a plethora of ornamental styles. Replicas of items that had once been rare and coveted articles of wonder became

'Since ornament is no longer a natural product of our culture, and consequently represents either backwardness or degeneration, the work of the ornament-maker is no longer paid for at the proper rate. The plight of the wood-carver and turner, the criminally low wages paid to embroideresses and lace-makers are well known. The ornament-maker must work for twenty hours to match the income of a modern worker who works eight hours.'

ADOLF LOOS, ORNAMENT AND CRIME
(Innsbruck, 1908).

22

9 Gombrich, *The Sense of Order*, 46.

readily available to those with a less discerning eye. While this was a welcome advent to the rising middle classes, it was in no way wondrous. There was no mystery in the source or production of these new material goods; in fact, the drudgery involved in their production was often too close at hand. From a contemporary perspective, it's difficult to lament this great social levelling, or to propose that only the wealthy deserve to have beautiful things, but I can't help but feel that on our march through the mechanical age, something was lost.

> 'Things are interesting because we care about them, and important because we need them. Had our perceptions no connexion with our pleasures, we should soon close our eyes on the world.'
>
> SANTAYANA, THE SENSE OF BEAUTY, 4.

Ornament and the wonder of man-made objects reached a major setback with the doctrine of Modernism. The move to rationalism and functionalism as the supreme goal deliberately left ornamentation behind.

To follow the Modernist ideal, if all objects and materials are immediately evident, if function achieves perfection in, say, the perfect fork or the functional building, then there is little room to wonder, seek and change. What is to wonder at when everything you see and use is completely evident, including its manufacture? Furthermore, to restrict function to physical use is to ignore the spiritual properties that can be experienced in things, and to deny imagination and pleasure as necessary properties in the enjoyment of life.

None of which is to say that there's no delight or inspiration in the perfection of form and the *je ne sais quoi* of volume and light. Myself, I am deeply respectful of Modernist design in architecture, furniture and graphics. But

23

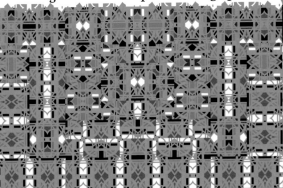

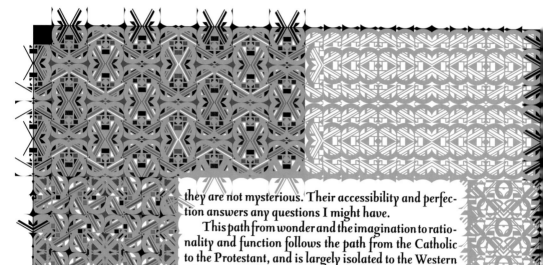

they are not mysterious. Their accessibility and perfection answers any questions I might have.

This path from wonder and the imagination to rationality and function follows the path from the Catholic to the Protestant, and is largely isolated to the Western Christian world.

WONDERS OF THE EAST

In Islam, intricate designs function quite differently in the presentation of the Qur'an. There, the intent of the elaborate artwork is to liberate the divine presence of the words. Muslims were expressive in their language and voice, speaking and chanting verses from memory, and they determined that the written word should 'be as powerful an experience for the eye as the memorized record is for the ear'.[10] Muslims are certainly not without their politics over ornament and what should or should not be represented; in fact, they are known for their aversion to the depiction of heavenly or earthly creatures, so as not to challenge God with the creation of living things or to encourage idolatry. But in this, there was also the desire not to stunt the imagination with the direct depiction of things – an interesting way to look at what we see as a restriction, but what they saw as a visual mechanism for the release of the imagination.

The beauty and intricacy of Islamic illumination, particularly as it developed around the fourteenth century, is unparalleled. The rhythm, harmony and structure of the pages, combined with the breathtakingly

24

10 Martin Lings, *Splendours of Qur'an Calligraphy and Illumination* (Liechtenstein, 2005), 15.

elegant script and extremely sophisticated design, sings with, in the words of Martin Lings, 'compose and inner rhythm ... unending melody and divine mathematics'.[11] In Islamic art, the function 'is parallel to that of the Revelation itself as a means of causing repercussions in the human soul in the direction of the Transcendent'.[12] So ornamentation is recognized as having an effective function. Maybe it's because of this that these arts have not been abandoned in contemporary Islamic religious works.

Where Islamic art is designed towards release of the word, Tibetan art is constructed as embodiment of the divine. Tibetans have no strictures against representing earthly or heavenly beings; on the contrary, the complex visuals, rife with symbolism, are created as dwelling places for the living presence of the Buddha. Their representation stimulates faith and aspiration, the intricate surrounds inspire the imagination through meditation. They are glorious representations of an exquisite world that 'corrects a people's view of reality from hostile to friendly, from scarce to bounteous, from chaotic and confusing to ordered, beautiful and illuminating'.[13]

In both the Islamic and Tibetan art, wonder works as a doorway to the imagination and, ultimately, to

'The significant factor in Islamic art is neither aversion to empty space nor a gratuitous use of geometric design, but a drive towards absolute sanctification. The superabundance of the sacred is such that it contains its own void. Muslim art moves onward in a secret veiled anguish that harbours in itself a mystical experience. Hence the arabesque, which expresses this anguish in decorative form. It holds the balance of line and colour to a point where they begin to ... vibrate in an interlaced tracery, and epigraphy and natural or geometric decoration are combined. This tracery holds the superabundance in check, yet marks a secret desire to lose itself ... On this voyage of celebration, the world delivers the soul of the believer to the anguish of the Invisible.'

ABDELKEBIR KHATIBI AND
MOHAMED SIJELMASSI,
THE SPLENDOUR OF ISLAMIC
CALLIGRAPHY (London, 1996), 170.

11 Lings, 16.

12 Ibid., 44.

13 Marylin M. Rhie and Robert A. F. Thurman, *Worlds of Transformation: Tibetan Art of Wisdom and Compassion* (New York, 1999), 31, 37.

transformation. Without doing exhaustive research into other religions, simply by looking at the visual cultures of many other societies, the Western world seems to be alone in binding wonder, ornament and craft into issues of morality.

CONTEMPORARY WONDER

Despite the struggles against modernization by Morris and the Arts and Crafts movement, the knowledge of craft in the West became all but extinct. Looking back from the twenty-first century to the intricate carpets, engraving, metalwork, carving, mosaics, calligraphy, and inlay created in previous centuries, it is difficult not to feel the wonder of the things and the people who made them.

In the late twentieth century, it was the imperfect and the handmade that inspired our awe: items of singularity that represent that most important and precious commodity, the investment of time and human energy. Beauty is, of course, in the eye of the beholder, but even without subjective judgement, things of great detail and monumental human effort do continue to amaze us. To wit, our fascination with the obsessives of outsider art – those mad detailists who labour away with pens, brushes or bits of glass – it's not necessarily the materials or the form per se, but the time spent in creating such complexity; we can feel the life emanating from it.

Currently, we may be living in the most wondrous age of all time. The computer, although made and operated by humans, has taken over the realm of magic. Those wizards of programming are their powerful masters, but the knowledge to control computer technology lies in the hands of the relatively few. For the rest of us, mysterious things happen – some of them pleasing, some confounding.

Contemporary architecture has benefited enormously from the magic of computing, and new architectural spaces can be full of wonder. Seemingly impossible buildings stand up, take strange shapes, tower above us, and expose fascinatingly complex skeletons and skins. New materials combine volume without heaviness, transparency and opacity, strength and flexibility. Buildings light up with moving displays of words and images transmitted from around the world. Machinery driven by computers allows us to shape materials, old and new, into previously impossible forms. The best of architecture today holds as much mystery and power as did the Gothic cathedrals of old. They share those enormous, impossible volumes, height and light that make us look up in awe.

Nature and science, too, are still essential sources of mystery and fascination, with enormous potential to lift us out of our petty pursuits and superstitions. Above all else, the advancements we have made in science are truly marvellous. We have discovered new worlds, creatures and ways of being; we are in an exploratory bonanza

'The prophets who forecast a sterile, uniform future were wrong, because they imagined a society shaped by impersonal laws of history and technology, divorced from individuality, pleasure and imagination.'

VIRGINIA I. POSTREL, THE SUBSTANCE OF STYLE: HOW THE RISE OF AESTHETIC VALUE IS REMAKING COMMERCE, CULTURE, AND CONSCIOUSNESS (New York, 2003), 33.

27

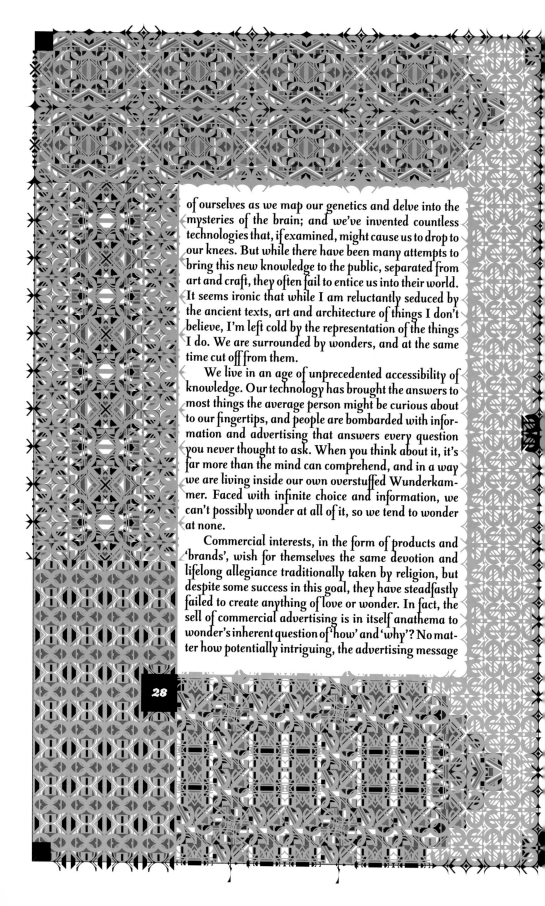

of ourselves as we map our genetics and delve into the mysteries of the brain; and we've invented countless technologies that, if examined, might cause us to drop to our knees. But while there have been many attempts to bring this new knowledge to the public, separated from art and craft, they often fail to entice us into their world. It seems ironic that while I am reluctantly seduced by the ancient texts, art and architecture of things I don't believe, I'm left cold by the representation of the things I do. We are surrounded by wonders, and at the same time cut off from them.

We live in an age of unprecedented accessibility of knowledge. Our technology has brought the answers to most things the average person might be curious about to our fingertips, and people are bombarded with information and advertising that answers every question you never thought to ask. When you think about it, it's far more than the mind can comprehend, and in a way we are living inside our own overstuffed Wunderkammer. Faced with infinite choice and information, we can't possibly wonder at all of it, so we tend to wonder at none.

Commercial interests, in the form of products and 'brands', wish for themselves the same devotion and lifelong allegiance traditionally taken by religion, but despite some success in this goal, they have steadfastly failed to create anything of love or wonder. In fact, the sell of commercial advertising is in itself anathema to wonder's inherent question of 'how' and 'why'? No matter how potentially intriguing, the advertising message is like a slap in the face at the end of a dream. Devotion to a product is motivated largely by status or from practical use, and while there are those who feel strongly enough to mark themselves in some way with a logo, I know of few marvellous works inspired by brand worship.

Despite the still-evident wonders of nature, our appreciation has become tainted with the desperate sorrow of impending loss. To watch a programme such as the BBC nature series *Planet Earth* is to be delighted and uplifted with joy and amazement, followed swiftly by fear and concern for the longevity of the wonders we've just seen. Still, many of us live in cities or towns where nearly everything is man-made and thoroughly explainable; even the infinitude of the night sky is invisible, washed away by city lights. For these people, nature has almost vanished, preserved and observed at a distance on TV.

Perhaps we're moving too fast to be inspired by what's around us. Our news, entertainment and learning are fed to us in increasingly smaller bites, which we thoughtlessly consume, each bite replaced by the next. We need time to make and time to pause and appreciate, but our rush to assimilate more impoverishes us spiritually and intellectually, and robs us of a deep connection with the world. While the religious lament the modern world's lack of connection with the gods, I lament our lack of wonder and loss of innocence.

If wonder is a childlike innocence, perhaps as we grow older as a society we lose our collective ability to feel it. To take for granted is the death of wonder. When we

take people, our environment and our lives for granted, our weariness and illusion of knowledge allows us to destroy the things our ancestors held so much in awe. As we televise the world and replicate it in theme parks and digital simulacra, we inure ourselves to the wonder of reality, and the magnificence of the world as we found it. We need to allow the mind to wander into its unnatural conclusions, surprising us with leaps of thought and the childish joy of unknowing. Curiosity, that once impious act that dares to question what was given, is the key to the fantastic.

To say 'I wonder' is to say 'I question; I ask.' The mind seeks. Sometimes it finds answers, sometimes it does not. We need wonder in order to keep moving and growing – to stay alive to the world. It gives us meaning and, in fact, makes us human.

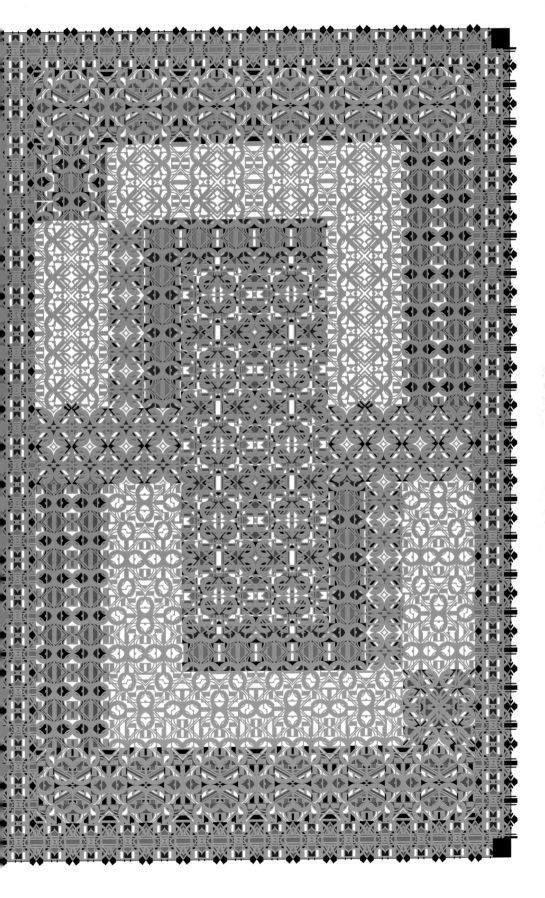

IN THE FALL of 2006 I was in Hollywood on business of a sort, with no intention of looking for stars. In fact, when it comes to Hollywood stars I have little to no interest, with one or two notable exceptions. But as it turned out, LA's Griffith Observatory had been newly refurbished, so I decided to go for a visit and do some real stargazing.

An observatory in LA seemed like a weird idea to me, but – much to my surprise – it was high on a hill and we got to look down on all the pollution instead of up through it, so that was a relief. And what a view it was.

Stars. You know, when we think of stars we tend to think of one or two shapes, a couple of different sizes, and that's about it. How wrong that is. Stars come in all sorts of different configurations, colours and shapes. Sometimes you're not even sure ... Is that thing a star? But once you get your head around it, if it's bright and twinkly, has points and is in the sky, it's probably a star.

Stars are actually big balls of gas powered by nuclear fusion, but fortunately for us, they look a lot prettier than that sounds. Stars are described by brightness, colour, size, age and number of points, among other things. When counting points on a star, just count the big ones that stick out; everything else is just stardust.

THREE- and four-pointed stars are rare. Above is the three-pointed star, *Envy #542766* (yes, I know, it sounds like a perfume), from the galaxy *I Zwicky 18*. The twin stars are *Castor* and *Pollux* from the constellation *Gemini*, which means they are energetic, charismatic and communicative – oops! that's astrology, not astronomy: two very different things. The red star is called *TVLM 513-46546* (a nicer name would be appropriate – perhaps *La Superba*? Oh wait, that's taken), which is a flare star that spins wildly every two days, making it a common reference in modern dance.

MOST STARS have five points. This is the shape we tend to think of when we think 'star'. But even here, note the differences in appearance between some simple five-pointed stars. Surprising, isn't it? The *North Star* (*Polaris*), above, appears above the North Pole and has blue tips from poor circulation. Who'd have thought that such an important star would be so plain? Well, it's only important to us, not to the rest of the universe – humans are incredibly egocentric. The blue-and-white star is the famous *Rigel*, the brightest star of Orion. *Rigel* has a habit of making appearances in TV and movies, often in disguise as a planet with a number after its name. Don't be fooled!

THERE ARE thousands of five-pointed stars that simply blow the mind with their intricacy. You and I just look up at the sky and see some little pinpricks of light, but if you take a really close look with a massive telescope, the stars reveal themselves to be incredibly unique and wonderful things. Look at that one directly below ... that's what I'm talking about when I say, 'What, is that a star?' That's *Sirius*, and it's a double star, where *Sirius A* is a hot blue-white and *Sirius B* is its resentful sister, a white dwarf. To the right of it, burning at 13,500 times brighter than our sun, is the blue supergiant *Menkib*, the hottest star visible to the naked eye. Sexy space! In the middle at the bottom is a very old white dwarf called *Blanche*, poor thing.

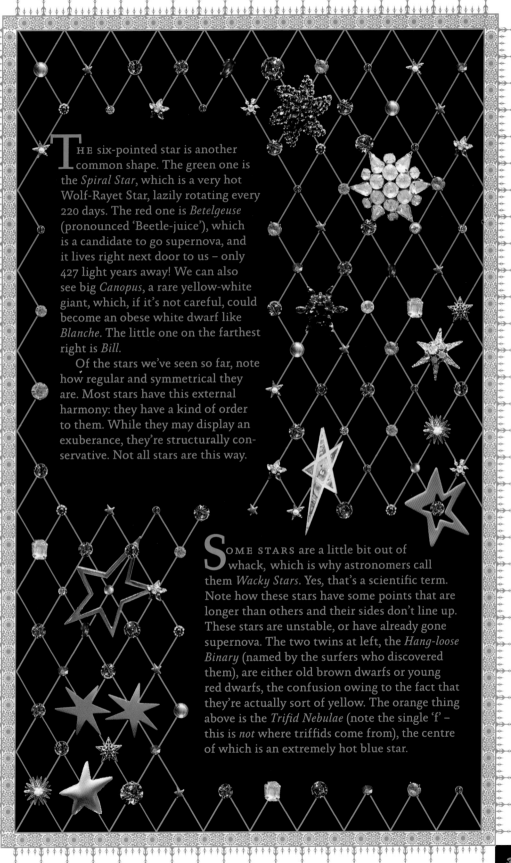

THE six-pointed star is another common shape. The green one is the *Spiral Star*, which is a very hot Wolf-Rayet Star, lazily rotating every 220 days. The red one is *Betelgeuse* (pronounced 'Beetle-juice'), which is a candidate to go supernova, and it lives right next door to us – only 427 light years away! We can also see big *Canopus*, a rare yellow-white giant, which, if it's not careful, could become an obese white dwarf like *Blanche*. The little one on the farthest right is *Bill*.

Of the stars we've seen so far, note how regular and symmetrical they are. Most stars have this external harmony: they have a kind of order to them. While they may display an exuberance, they're structurally conservative. Not all stars are this way.

SOME STARS are a little bit out of whack, which is why astronomers call them *Wacky Stars*. Yes, that's a scientific term. Note how these stars have some points that are longer than others and their sides don't line up. These stars are unstable, or have already gone supernova. The two twins at left, the *Hang-loose Binary* (named by the surfers who discovered them), are either old brown dwarfs or young red dwarfs, the confusion owing to the fact that they're actually sort of yellow. The orange thing above is the *Trifid Nebulae* (note the single 'f' – this is *not* where triffids come from), the centre of which is an extremely hot blue star.

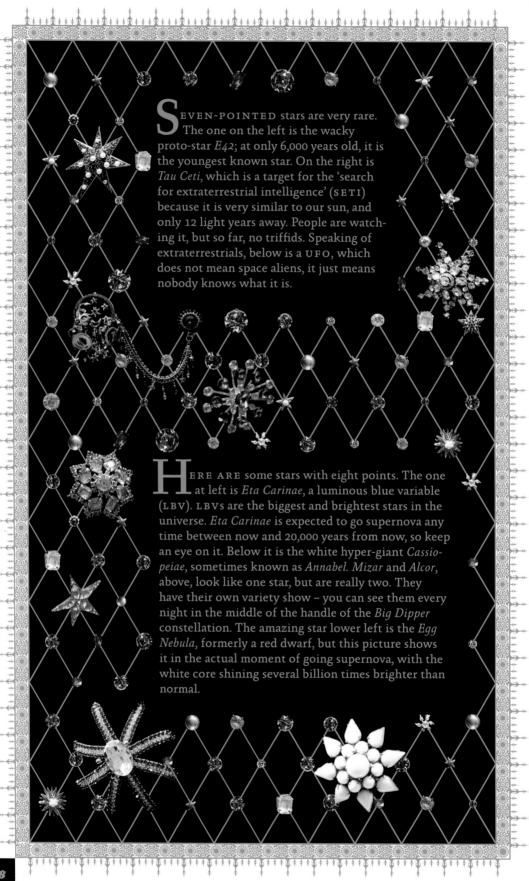

SEVEN-POINTED stars are very rare. The one on the left is the wacky proto-star *E42*; at only 6,000 years old, it is the youngest known star. On the right is *Tau Ceti*, which is a target for the 'search for extraterrestrial intelligence' (SETI) because it is very similar to our sun, and only 12 light years away. People are watching it, but so far, no triffids. Speaking of extraterrestrials, below is a UFO, which does not mean space aliens, it just means nobody knows what it is.

HERE ARE some stars with eight points. The one at left is *Eta Carinae*, a luminous blue variable (LBV). LBVs are the biggest and brightest stars in the universe. *Eta Carinae* is expected to go supernova any time between now and 20,000 years from now, so keep an eye on it. Below it is the white hyper-giant *Cassiopeiae*, sometimes known as *Annabel*. *Mizar* and *Alcor*, above, look like one star, but are really two. They have their own variety show – you can see them every night in the middle of the handle of the *Big Dipper* constellation. The amazing star lower left is the *Egg Nebula*, formerly a red dwarf, but this picture shows it in the actual moment of going supernova, with the white core shining several billion times brighter than normal.

WE COULD NOT find any nine-pointed stars. Mr Astronomer (*not his name!* I was so impolite, and forgot to ask him) said he's seen some, but just couldn't find any that day. He did find the 10-pointed yellow super-giant, *Wezen*, and this previously undiscovered 11-pointed star! We named it right then and there: *Bantjes*. It's a hot blue-white supergiant, and I think it's the most beautiful star in the galaxy.

SOMETIMES you think you're looking at a single star, but really it's a whole group of little stars collected together in a small space ... well, if you consider four million times the sun to be 'small'. At left is *Fomalhaut*, a very inter-esting white star surrounded by dust and in the process of forming planets, which you can see here. Below it is a cluster that shows evidence of rare blue stragglers on the edges. And the big green one is the superstar cluster *Ego*. Directly below that is a big, bright globular cluster called *Omega Centauri*, which contains millions of stars but is actually part of the *Milky Way* galaxy. And watch out! That swirling red thing is a *black hole*.

BELOW are starbursts – not the bad advertising kind of starburst, these are the good kind! Starbursts have a multitude of extra-long rays because they're actually exploding! In these images, you can even see the chunks of the original star that are flying off from the core. They're incredibly exciting, which is why they're used in advertising.

Telescopes are amazing.

HERE ARE some images of the star closest to us in the galaxy, our very own sun, which is a single, yellow star that's 4.6 billion years old. At the Griffith Observatory they have a triple-mirrored tracking device called a coelostat (not to be confused with a coelacanth), which follows the sun and collects the light for their three solar telescopes. Depending on the filters they use to view it, the sun can appear very different. These are just a few views. Note the little image where it looks like our sun is a red dwarf. Our sun is *not* a red dwarf! We would be in serious shit if it was. That's just a view of it in infrared light.

THE MOON was in its crescent phase while I was there. Shown here are a number of different views; they look so different because they've been 'enhanced' with hand-tinting to bring out certain special things that moon scientists are interested in. It's amazing how recognizable it is, despite the slightly different forms. You'd be a lunatic to think it was a C, or insect pincers, or a half-eaten doughnut. The moon is very shiny and often reflects images of stars on its surface. Also shown is the 'man in the moon'. I didn't actually see this; these are archival photos. Mr Astronomer was very cagey about the whole thing.

Now this is really interesting. On very rare occasions, due to a disturbance in the atmosphere, it can appear as though a star is passing in front of the moon. This is, of course, impossible, as stars are very big and much further away than the moon, but these exciting images show the phenomenon clearly. Sometimes the illusion is so intense, it appears as though a star actually eclipses the moon! At the top left is our old friend *Tau Ceti*, the seven-pointed star. To the far right of it is a double-optical shift; and note the one that looks like a starburst, but is really just a very sparkly star interfering with the moon rays for this amazing special effect.

Here on the left is a super rare image taken during a summer when it was really hot down here on Earth, and California was alight with forest fires ... well, that's the cheese melting right off the moon! I kid you not.

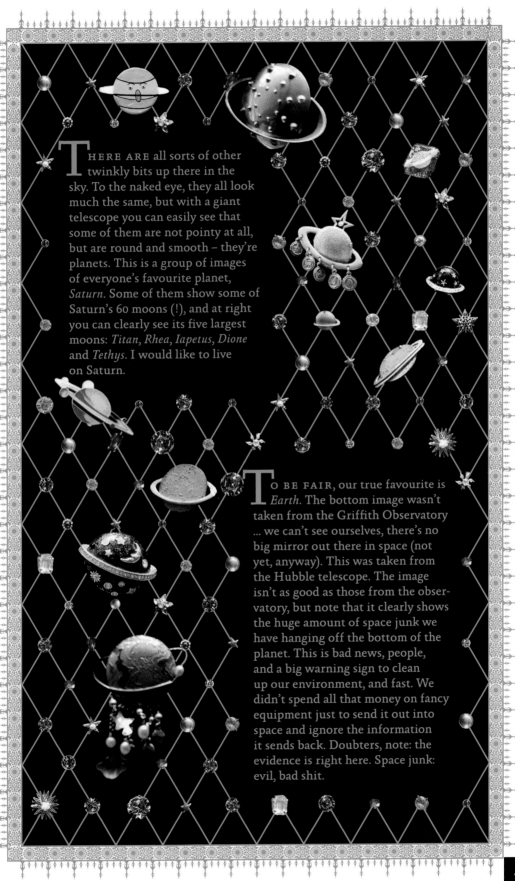

THERE ARE all sorts of other twinkly bits up there in the sky. To the naked eye, they all look much the same, but with a giant telescope you can easily see that some of them are not pointy at all, but are round and smooth – they're planets. This is a group of images of everyone's favourite planet, *Saturn*. Some of them show some of Saturn's 60 moons (!), and at right you can clearly see its five largest moons: *Titan, Rhea, Iapetus, Dione* and *Tethys*. I would like to live on Saturn.

TO BE FAIR, our true favourite is *Earth*. The bottom image wasn't taken from the Griffith Observatory … we can't see ourselves, there's no big mirror out there in space (not yet, anyway). This was taken from the Hubble telescope. The image isn't as good as those from the observatory, but note that it clearly shows the huge amount of space junk we have hanging off the bottom of the planet. This is bad news, people, and a big warning sign to clean up our environment, and fast. We didn't spend all that money on fancy equipment just to send it out into space and ignore the information it sends back. Doubters, note: the evidence is right here. Space junk: evil, bad shit.

THERE is a lot of flotsam and jetsam flying around out there in space, and not all of it was put there by us. We call these beautiful things shooting stars, but actually they're meteors, or meteoroids. The really bright ones are called *Fireballs*, while the dull ones are called *Dimwits*. Sometimes they fall to Earth and wipe out forests to make craters, but that's pretty rare. By the time they get here, they're just ugly hunks of rock that we call meteorites, but out there in space ... well look at that. They are just lovely.

I REMEMBER when, in 1986, *Halley's Comet* came around for a visit, and it was big news and excitement in my spot on the prairies. Well, here it is again. It's so great to see it's OK and still travelling around the galaxy. Humans have been recording it for about 24 centuries, and it comes to visit every 75 or 76 years. If you're reading this in 2061, you might want to keep an eye out for it in the sky.

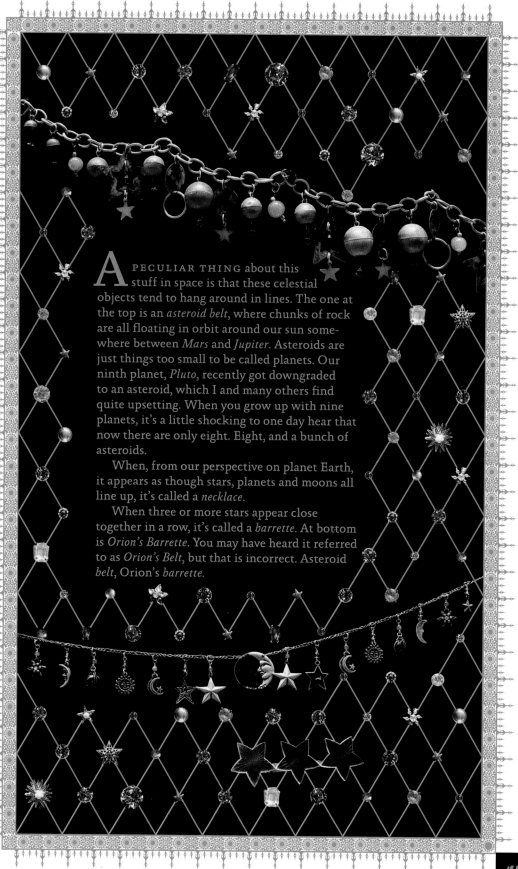

A PECULIAR THING about this stuff in space is that these celestial objects tend to hang around in lines. The one at the top is an *asteroid belt*, where chunks of rock are all floating in orbit around our sun somewhere between *Mars* and *Jupiter*. Asteroids are just things too small to be called planets. Our ninth planet, *Pluto*, recently got downgraded to an asteroid, which I and many others find quite upsetting. When you grow up with nine planets, it's a little shocking to one day hear that now there are only eight. Eight, and a bunch of asteroids.

When, from our perspective on planet Earth, it appears as though stars, planets and moons all line up, it's called a *necklace*.

When three or more stars appear close together in a row, it's called a *barrette*. At bottom is *Orion's Barrette*. You may have heard it referred to as *Orion's Belt*, but that is incorrect. Asteroid *belt*, Orion's *barrette*.

STARS form in *galaxies*. The smallest are irregular galaxies, which are quite shapeless. Spiral galaxies are the most common, and the really big ones are elliptical. Ours, called the *Milky Way*, is a spiral galaxy with two arms. Each arm is called a bracelet, like the one in the centre. (We can't see our galaxy here, because we're *inside* it.)

HERE ARE a few great shots of galaxies that are far away. You can tell galaxies from star clusters because they're much bigger and they often have those bracelets that spiral outwards from the centre. It looks like they're swirling round and round ... sort of hypnotizing. Below are the *Pinwheel* and *Socialite* galaxies.

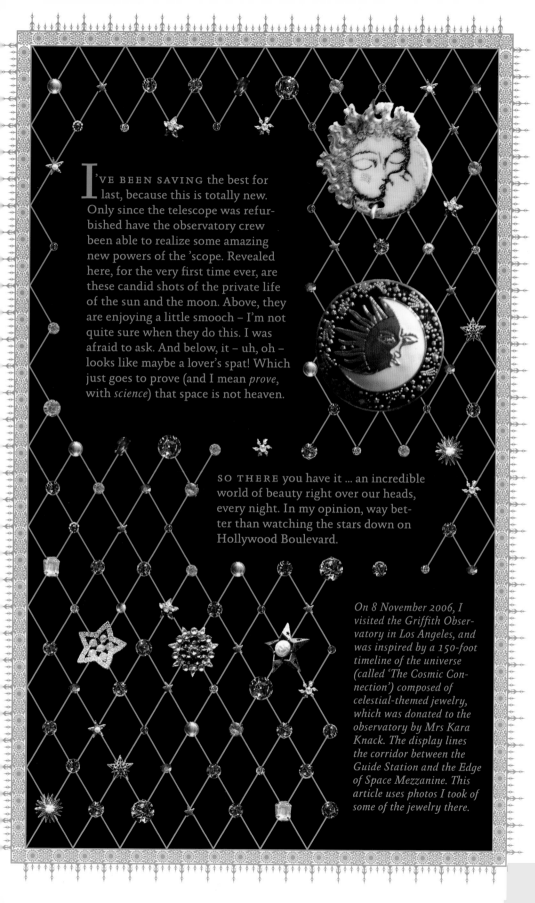

I'VE BEEN SAVING the best for last, because this is totally new. Only since the telescope was refurbished have the observatory crew been able to realize some amazing new powers of the 'scope. Revealed here, for the very first time ever, are these candid shots of the private life of the sun and the moon. Above, they are enjoying a little smooch – I'm not quite sure when they do this. I was afraid to ask. And below, it – uh, oh – looks like maybe a lover's spat! Which just goes to prove (and I mean *prove*, with *science*) that space is not heaven.

SO THERE you have it ... an incredible world of beauty right over our heads, every night. In my opinion, way better than watching the stars down on Hollywood Boulevard.

On 8 November 2006, I visited the Griffith Observatory in Los Angeles, and was inspired by a 150-foot timeline of the universe (called 'The Cosmic Connection') composed of celestial-themed jewelry, which was donated to the observatory by Mrs Kara Knack. The display lines the corridor between the Guide Station and the Edge of Space Mezzanine. This article uses photos I took of some of the jewelry there.

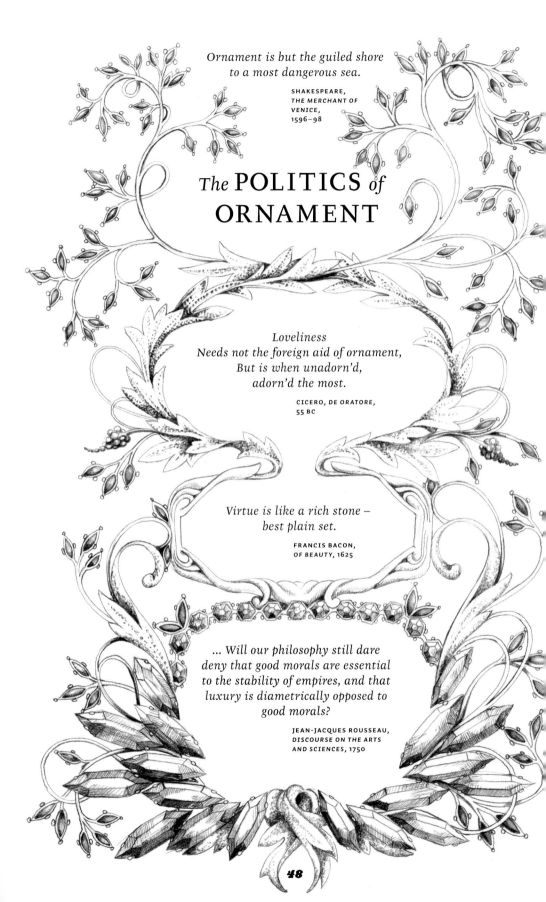

Ornament is but the guiled shore
to a most dangerous sea.

SHAKESPEARE,
THE MERCHANT OF
VENICE,
1596–98

The POLITICS of ORNAMENT

Loveliness
Needs not the foreign aid of ornament,
But is when unadorn'd,
adorn'd the most.

CICERO, DE ORATORE,
55 BC

Virtue is like a rich stone –
best plain set.

FRANCIS BACON,
OF BEAUTY, 1625

... Will our philosophy still dare
deny that good morals are essential
to the stability of empires, and that
luxury is diametrically opposed to
good morals?

JEAN-JACQUES ROUSSEAU,
DISCOURSE ON THE ARTS
AND SCIENCES, 1750

On the stucco
are monsters rather than
definite representations taken from
definite things. Instead of columns
there rise up stalks; instead of gables,
striped panels with curled leaves and
volutes. Candelabra uphold pictured
shrines and above the summits of
these, clusters of thin stalks rise
from their roots in tendrils with little
figures seated upon them
at random. Again, slender stalks
with heads of men and animals
attached to half the body.
Such things neither are, nor can be,
nor have been. On these lines the new
fashions compel bad judges
to condemn good craftsmanship
for dullness ... When people view
these falsehoods, they approve
rather than condemn.

VITRUVIUS,
DE ARCHITECTURA,
C. 27 BC

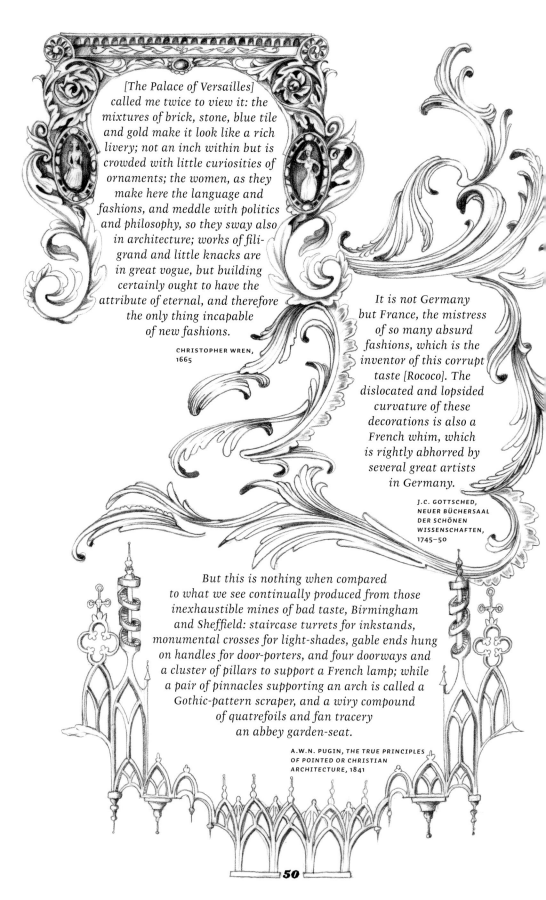

[The Palace of Versailles] called me twice to view it: the mixtures of brick, stone, blue tile and gold make it look like a rich livery; not an inch within but is crowded with little curiosities of ornaments; the women, as they make here the language and fashions, and meddle with politics and philosophy, so they sway also in architecture; works of fili-grand and little knacks are in great vogue, but building certainly ought to have the attribute of eternal, and therefore the only thing incapable of new fashions.

CHRISTOPHER WREN, 1665

It is not Germany but France, the mistress of so many absurd fashions, which is the inventor of this corrupt taste [Rococo]. The dislocated and lopsided curvature of these decorations is also a French whim, which is rightly abhorred by several great artists in Germany.

J.C. GOTTSCHED, NEUER BÜCHERSAAL DER SCHÖNEN WISSENSCHAFTEN, 1745–50

But this is nothing when compared to what we see continually produced from those inexhaustible mines of bad taste, Birmingham and Sheffield: staircase turrets for inkstands, monumental crosses for light-shades, gable ends hung on handles for door-porters, and four doorways and a cluster of pillars to support a French lamp; while a pair of pinnacles supporting an arch is called a Gothic-pattern scraper, and a wiry compound of quatrefoils and fan tracery an abbey garden-seat.

A.W.N. PUGIN, THE TRUE PRINCIPLES OF POINTED OR CHRISTIAN ARCHITECTURE, 1841

The means of multiplying elegant forms by punches, squeezes, moulds, types, dies, casts and like contrivances, enables us to produce objects with a sufficient degree of beauty to satisfy the general fancy for art or ornament, but so as to kill all life and freedom. A permanent glut of pseudo-art is created; the multitudes are overfed with a superabundance of trashy food, and their appetite will never desire any better nutriment.

SIR FRANCIS PALGRAVE,
THE FINE ARTS IN
FLORENCE, 1840

... An incongruous mix of ornament and realism ... [showing] the same ignorance of that basic need in creating patterns, the integrity of the surface, and the same sickening vulgarity in detail.

NIKOLAUS PEVSNER,
PIONEERS OF THE
MODERN MOVEMENT,
1936

We are forced to step over bulging scrolls and into large, unpleasantly realistic flowers.

PEVSNER, PIONEERS OF
THE MODERN MOVEMENT,
1936

Forms which are not
taken from natural objects
must be ugly.

JOHN RUSKIN, THE
SEVEN LAMPS OF
ARCHITECTURE, 1849

Everything made by
man's hands has a form,
which must be either beautiful or
ugly; beautiful if it is in accord with
Nature, and helps her;
ugly if it is discordant with
Nature, and thwarts her;
it cannot be indifferent.

WILLIAM MORRIS,
THE LESSER ARTS, 1882

Set yourselves
as much as possible against
all machine work (this to all men).
But if you have to design for machine
work, at least let your design
show clearly what it is. Make it
mechanical with a vengeance,
at the same time as simple as
possible. Don't try, for instance
to make a printed plate look like a
hand-painted one: make it something
which no one would try if he were
painting by hand.

WILLIAM MORRIS,
ART AND THE BEAUTY OF
THE EARTH, 1899

Always look for invention first ...
demand no refinement of execution
where there is no thought,
for that is slaves' work,
unredeemed. Rather, choose rough
work than smooth work, so only
that the practical purpose be
answered, and never imagine there
is reason to be proud of anything
that may be accomplished by
patience and sandpaper.

JOHN RUSKIN,
THE STONES OF VENICE,
1851–53

All very neat,
finished, and perfect form
in glass is barbarous ...
The more wild,
extravagant, and
grotesque in their
gracefulness the forms
are, the better.
No material is so adapted
or giving full ply to the
imagination, but it must
not be wrought with
refinement ... we are
also frankly to admit its
fragility, and therefore
not to waste much time
upon it, nor put any real
art into it when intended
for daily use.
No workman ought
ever to spend more
than an hour in
the making of any
glass vessel.

RUSKIN,
THE STONES
OF VENICE,
1851–53

Ornamented
objects appear truly
unaesthetic if they
have been executed in
the best material, with
the highest degree of
meticulous detail, and
if they have required a
long production time
... The modern man
who holds ornament
sacred as the sign of
artistic achievement
of past epochs
will immediately
recognize the tortured,
laboriously extracted
and pathological
nature of modern
ornament.

ADOLF LOOS,
ORNAMENT AND
CRIME, 1908

53

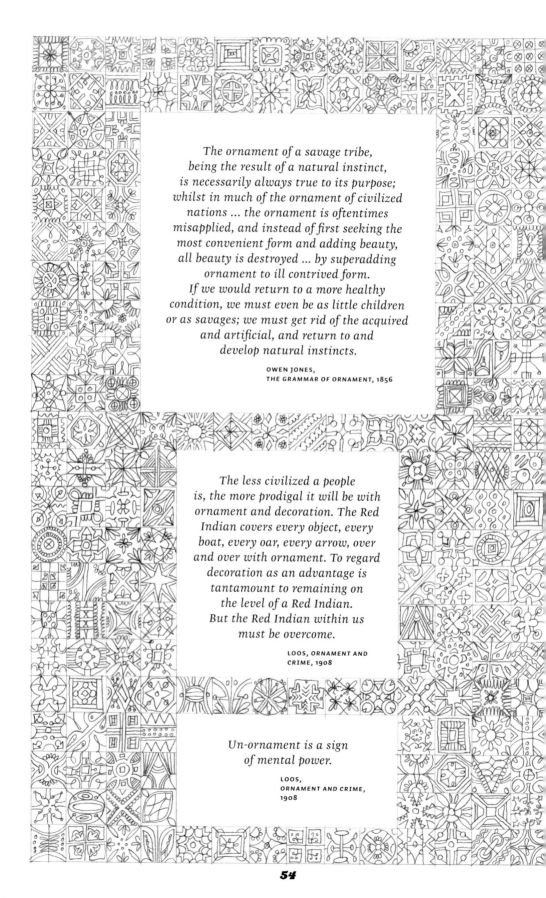

The ornament of a savage tribe,
being the result of a natural instinct,
is necessarily always true to its purpose;
whilst in much of the ornament of civilized
nations ... the ornament is oftentimes
misapplied, and instead of first seeking the
most convenient form and adding beauty,
all beauty is destroyed ... by superadding
ornament to ill contrived form.
If we would return to a more healthy
condition, we must even be as little children
or as savages; we must get rid of the acquired
and artificial, and return to and
develop natural instincts.

OWEN JONES,
THE GRAMMAR OF ORNAMENT, 1856

The less civilized a people
is, the more prodigal it will be with
ornament and decoration. The Red
Indian covers every object, every
boat, every oar, every arrow, over
and over with ornament. To regard
decoration as an advantage is
tantamount to remaining on
the level of a Red Indian.
But the Red Indian within us
must be overcome.

LOOS, ORNAMENT AND
CRIME, 1908

Un-ornament is a sign
of mental power.

LOOS,
ORNAMENT AND CRIME,
1908

Less is more.

LUDWIG MIES VAN DER ROHE

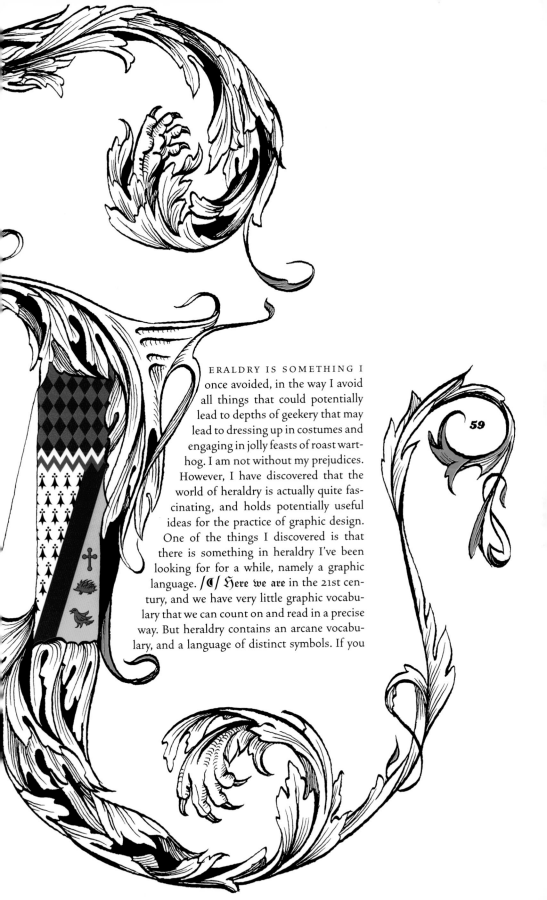

ERALDRY IS SOMETHING I once avoided, in the way I avoid all things that could potentially lead to depths of geekery that may lead to dressing up in costumes and engaging in jolly feasts of roast wart-hog. I am not without my prejudices. However, I have discovered that the world of heraldry is actually quite fascinating, and holds potentially useful ideas for the practice of graphic design. One of the things I discovered is that there is something in heraldry I've been looking for for a while, namely a graphic language. /𝕮/ Here we are in the 21st century, and we have very little graphic vocabulary that we can count on and read in a precise way. But heraldry contains an arcane vocabulary, and a language of distinct symbols. If you

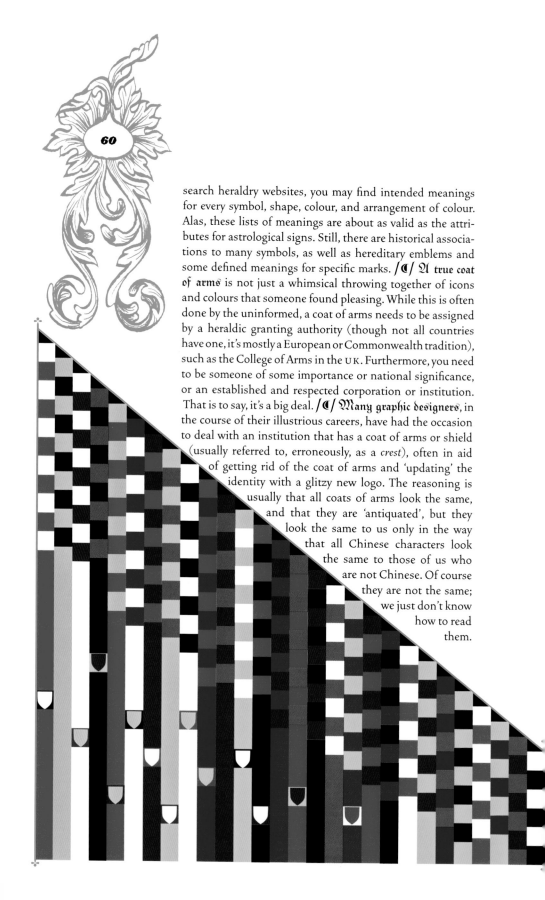

search heraldry websites, you may find intended meanings for every symbol, shape, colour, and arrangement of colour. Alas, these lists of meanings are about as valid as the attributes for astrological signs. Still, there are historical associations to many symbols, as well as hereditary emblems and some defined meanings for specific marks. /⟨/ 𝔄 true coat of arms is not just a whimsical throwing together of icons and colours that someone found pleasing. While this is often done by the uninformed, a coat of arms needs to be assigned by a heraldic granting authority (though not all countries have one, it's mostly a European or Commonwealth tradition), such as the College of Arms in the UK. Furthermore, you need to be someone of some importance or national significance, or an established and respected corporation or institution. That is to say, it's a big deal. /⟨/ 𝔐any graphic designers, in the course of their illustrious careers, have had the occasion to deal with an institution that has a coat of arms or shield (usually referred to, erroneously, as a *crest*), often in aid of getting rid of the coat of arms and 'updating' the identity with a glitzy new logo. The reasoning is usually that all coats of arms look the same, and that they are 'antiquated', but they look the same to us only in the way that all Chinese characters look the same to those of us who are not Chinese. Of course they are not the same; we just don't know how to read them.

HERALDRY HAS A WEALTH of terminology to describe graphic material in a way that could actually be quite useful. This language of heraldry is called *blazon*. There are names for each part of the coat of arms; for the different types and shapes of shield (*escutcheons*); for all the supporting parts of the coat of arms and shield, their positions and directions; for colours and patterns; and for all the other elements that go on the shield, plus their positions and directions. I'll cover enough to give you the general idea. /¶/ 𝕮𝖔𝖑𝖔𝖚𝖗𝖘 𝖆𝖗𝖊 𝖈𝖆𝖑𝖑𝖊𝖉 *tinctures* and come in three categories: metals (gold and silver, represented as yellow and white); furs (a spotted look, usually reminiscent of ermine and with a number of named variations); and colours (red, blue, black, green and purple). Tinctures are usually referred to by their French names (*or, argent, azure, gules,* etc.), but I will stick to English. Also, there are rules about how tinctures are used, rules that were designed to allow maximum visibility – very practical, as these emblems were often used on battlefields and you really needed to be able to see and read the graphics at a distance. On a shield, a metal icon may not be placed on a metal background, but only on a colour; similarly, a colour icon may only be placed on a metal or fur background. So you can't have a green gryphon on a blue background, it must be on white or yellow. And you can't have a yellow lion on a white background,

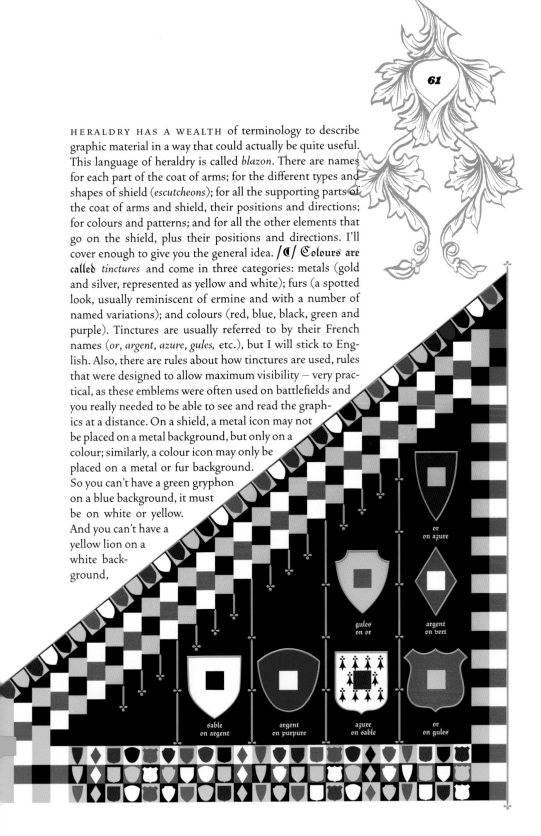

or
on azure

gules
on or

argent
on vert

sable
on argent

argent
on purpure

azure
on sable

or
on gules

it must be on one of the colours. *Visibility and clarity.* ❧
The background of the shield is called the *ground*, and it can be divided into a number of different *divisions* (divisions don't have to follow the metal/colour rule as they are considered to be beside each other). Left and right are described as *dexter* and *sinister*, though confusingly, sinister is to the left of the bearer of arms but to the right of the viewer. So sinister, which actually means left, is right, and dexter is left as we look at the arms. That's a detail that could use some updating. ❧ Any element that sits on the shield is called a *charge*, and the most basic of these are the *ordinaires*: simple shapes that come to the full edges of the shield. A horizontal bar is an ordinaire called a *fess* (unless it takes the full top of the shield, in which case it is the *chief*). A horizontal division across the middle is described as *party per fess* (the way of the fess), and things that run across the middle in a horizontal row are described as *fesswise*. A vertical bar is a *pale*, a vertical division in half is a *party per pale*, and things that run in a column down that line are *palewise*. Got it? An upside-down V bar is a *chevron*, and when you flip it the other way it becomes a *chevron inverted*. A diagonal bar that runs from top left to bottom right (as we view

fess
& charges fesswise

bend
sinister

bend
dexter

chevron

pale

chevron
inverted

quartering
(party per cross)

chief
over party per pale

party per
bend sinister

party per saltire

embattled

wavy

nebuly

dancetté

it) is a *bend* (leading to *per bend* and *bendwise*), and when it goes from top right to bottom left, it's a *bend sinister*. There are many more shapes (such as *pall*, *pile*, *canton*, *fret*, *flaunches*, etc.), but this will do for now. /❡/ There are also names for the shapes and edges of the ordinaires: zigzags are *indented*, or *dancetté*; *wavy* is, obviously, wavy; *nebuly* resembles the pieces of a jigsaw puzzle; *embattled* is like the battlements atop a castle. There are many other divisions, ordinaires and edges. But I will spare you. /❡/ OK, you've got the ground, you've got the division and/or the ordinaires, and on top of that you have a whole shitload of little symbols, sometimes called *mobile charges* because they are not restricted to size or position. These range from simple shapes like *lozenges* (diamonds), *roundels* (circles), *stars*, *crosses*, etc., to more pictorial elements such as plants, objects, humans and animals. All of these have some symbolic meaning (though not necessarily the kind you can look up in a reference book), or sometimes include a graphic pun on the name of the bearer — a device called *canting arms*. (An example of canting arms would be Paul Rand's 'IBM', represented by an eye, a bee and an M.) /❡/ Different types of shapes and ways of changing those

63

shapes are also identified. A solid shape can be *voided* (outlined) or *pierced* (with a round hole). A diamond shape is a *lozenge*; a lozenge that is voided is a *mascle*; a lozenge pierced is a *rustre*. There are hundreds of different types of crosses, many of them named. The names can also be used as adjectives. *Chequy* describes a field covered with small squares of alternate tinctures, and *lozengy* refers to a field covered in lozenges (cute!). /❦/ 𝕱urthermore, the animals take various positions and even have names for the positions of their bodies and body parts, which can vary depending on the animal. For instance: *rampant* refers to a beast of prey on its hind legs; *passant* is in a walking position with one forepaw raised; *passant reguardant* is walking but looking back; *passant repassant* is when two animals are walking past each other in opposite directions; *rampant sejant* is sitting with the forelegs raised. When animal parts are coloured differently from the animal, they are called *hoofed* or *maned* or *legged*, etc. *Despectant* describes animals looking downwards. *Embrued* refers to drops of blood falling upon or from something. And here's a handy one: *decked* is when the feathers of a bird are trimmed at the edges with a small line of colour that's different from the rest of the body. This, too, goes on and on.

Goat erased

Frog rampant

Giraffe statant reguardant

Hello lion guardant

Polar bear sejant

Winged donkey segreant

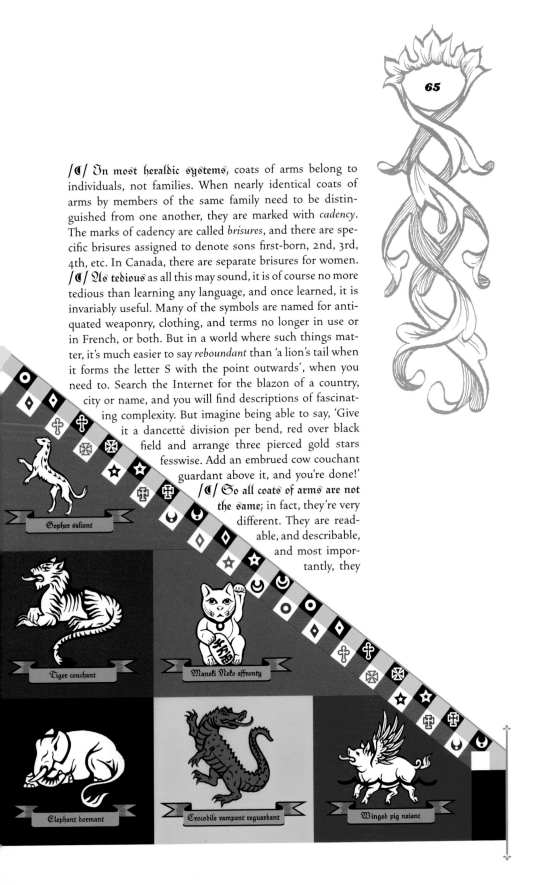

/€/ In most heraldic systems, coats of arms belong to individuals, not families. When nearly identical coats of arms by members of the same family need to be distinguished from one another, they are marked with *cadency*. The marks of cadency are called *brisures*, and there are specific brisures assigned to denote sons first-born, 2nd, 3rd, 4th, etc. In Canada, there are separate brisures for women. /€/ As tedious as all this may sound, it is of course no more tedious than learning any language, and once learned, it is invariably useful. Many of the symbols are named for antiquated weaponry, clothing, and terms no longer in use or in French, or both. But in a world where such things matter, it's much easier to say *reboundant* than 'a lion's tail when it forms the letter S with the point outwards', when you need to. Search the Internet for the blazon of a country, city or name, and you will find descriptions of fascinating complexity. But imagine being able to say, 'Give it a dancetté division per bend, red over black field and arrange three pierced gold stars fesswise. Add an embrued cow couchant guardant above it, and you're done!' /€/ So all coats of arms are not the same; in fact, they're very different. They are readable, and describable, and most importantly, they

Gopher salient

Tiger couchant

Maneki Neko affronty

Elephant dormant

Crocodile rampant reguardant

Winged pig naiant

mean something. Not only do they tell us something about the owner, but they tell us about their history and potential relationship to others. /⁋/ As mentioned earlier, you have to apply to get a coat of arms. But also, you can't just draw one up yourself. From the Canadian Heraldic Authority:

> Once the processing fee has been paid, the herald, a specialist in the field of emblematic design, begins work with the petitioner to determine the elements of a possible design, which must follow the rules of heraldry.[1]

And from the College of Arms, in Britain:

> The Kings of Arms have full discretion over the design of the armorial bearings they grant, but the wishes of the applicant are taken into account as fully as possible. The officer of arms who is acting for the petitioner will discuss with him or her the allusions and references he or she would like made in the design. Simplicity and boldness make for the best heraldic design and it is a mistake to seek the inclusion of too many references. The officer will, through his experience and knowledge of many thousands of coats of arms, be able to warn the petitioner of what is heraldically trite. The design must be proper heraldry and be distinct from all previous arms on record at the College.[2]

There is a lot in those two descriptions to warm the cockles of any graphic designer's heart, not the least of which is the

1. Canadian Heraldic Authority, 'Granting Armorial Bearings in Canada: Coats of Arms, Flags and Badges – Procedure Guide' (Ottawa, 2006), 6; http://archive.gg.ca/heraldry.

2. College of Arms, 'About the College of Arms: The Granting of Arms', www.college-of-arms.gov.uk.

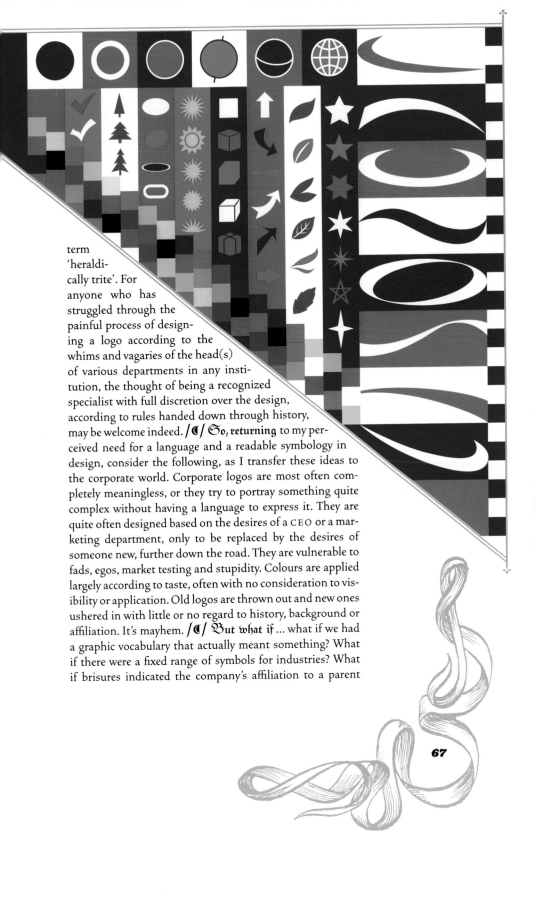

term 'heraldi- cally trite'. For anyone who has struggled through the painful process of design- ing a logo according to the whims and vagaries of the head(s) of various departments in any insti- tution, the thought of being a recognized specialist with full discretion over the design, according to rules handed down through history, may be welcome indeed. /❆/ So, returning to my per- ceived need for a language and a readable symbology in design, consider the following, as I transfer these ideas to the corporate world. Corporate logos are most often com- pletely meaningless, or they try to portray something quite complex without having a language to express it. They are quite often designed based on the desires of a CEO or a mar- keting department, only to be replaced by the desires of someone new, further down the road. They are vulnerable to fads, egos, market testing and stupidity. Colours are applied largely according to taste, often with no consideration to vis- ibility or application. Old logos are thrown out and new ones ushered in with little or no regard to history, background or affiliation. It's mayhem. /❆/ But what if ... what if we had a graphic vocabulary that actually meant something? What if there were a fixed range of symbols for industries? What if brisures indicated the company's affiliation to a parent

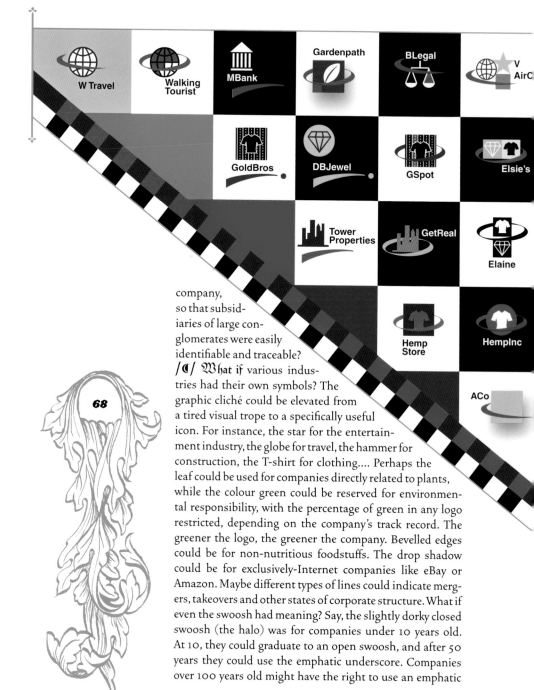

company,
so that subsid-
iaries of large con-
glomerates were easily
identifiable and traceable?
¶ What if various industries had their own symbols? The
graphic cliché could be elevated from
a tired visual trope to a specifically useful
icon. For instance, the star for the entertainment industry, the globe for travel, the hammer for
construction, the T-shirt for clothing.... Perhaps the
leaf could be used for companies directly related to plants,
while the colour green could be reserved for environmental responsibility, with the percentage of green in any logo
restricted, depending on the company's track record. The
greener the logo, the greener the company. Bevelled edges
could be for non-nutritious foodstuffs. The drop shadow
could be for exclusively-Internet companies like eBay or
Amazon. Maybe different types of lines could indicate merg-
ers, takeovers and other states of corporate structure. What if
even the swoosh had meaning? Say, the slightly dorky closed
swoosh (the halo) was for companies under 10 years old.
At 10, they could graduate to an open swoosh, and after 50
years they could use the emphatic underscore. Companies
over 100 years old might have the right to use an emphatic

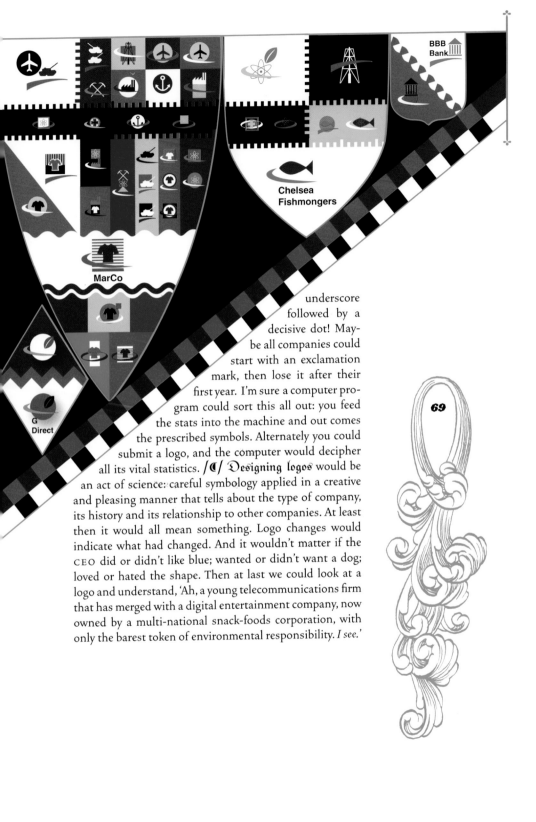

Chelsea
Fishmongers

MarCo

G
Direct

BBB
Bank

underscore followed by a decisive dot! Maybe all companies could start with an exclamation mark, then lose it after their first year. I'm sure a computer program could sort this all out: you feed the stats into the machine and out comes the prescribed symbols. Alternately you could submit a logo, and the computer would decipher all its vital statistics. ¶ Designing logos would be an act of science: careful symbology applied in a creative and pleasing manner that tells about the type of company, its history and its relationship to other companies. At least then it would all mean something. Logo changes would indicate what had changed. And it wouldn't matter if the CEO did or didn't like blue; wanted or didn't want a dog; loved or hated the shape. Then at last we could look at a logo and understand, 'Ah, a young telecommunications firm that has merged with a digital entertainment company, now owned by a multi-national snack-foods corporation, with only the barest token of environmental responsibility. *I see.*'

69

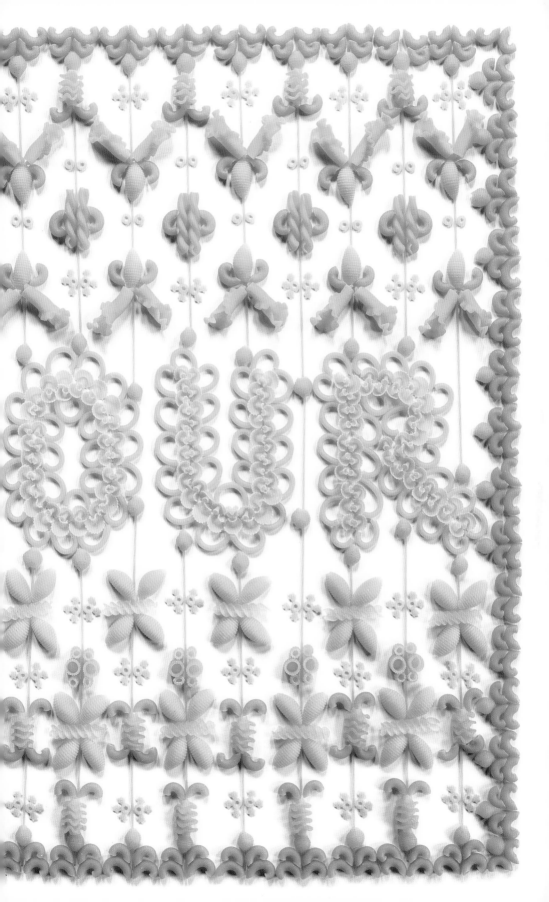

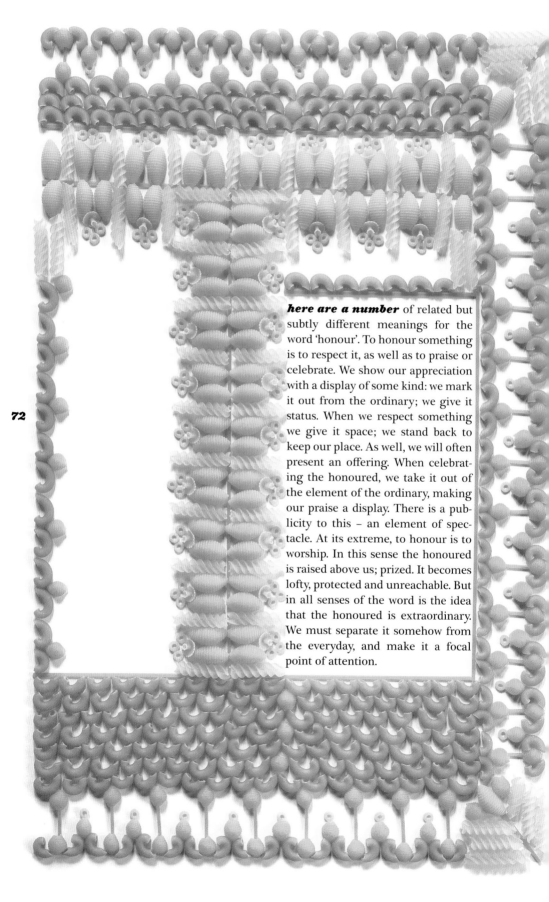

here are a number of related but subtly different meanings for the word 'honour'. To honour something is to respect it, as well as to praise or celebrate. We show our appreciation with a display of some kind: we mark it out from the ordinary; we give it status. When we respect something we give it space; we stand back to keep our place. As well, we will often present an offering. When celebrating the honoured, we take it out of the element of the ordinary, making our praise a display. There is a publicity to this – an element of spectacle. At its extreme, to honour is to worship. In this sense the honoured is raised above us; prized. It becomes lofty, protected and unreachable. But in all senses of the word is the idea that the honoured is extraordinary. We must separate it somehow from the everyday, and make it a focal point of attention.

In design, there is an oft-repeated phrase, 'honour the text', which is invoked as an entreaty to set text as cleanly and legibly as possible, and to put the content before the context. The design implication is 'the simpler, the better', and the lesson for designers is that the design should be the servant to the master of content. The designer's job is only to clear the path, and do nothing that would detract from the focus of the text.

> Imagine that you have before you a flagon of wine ... You have two goblets before you. One is of solid gold, wrought in the most exquisite patterns. The other is of crystal-clear glass, thin as a bubble, and as transparent. Pour and drink; and according to your choice of goblet, I shall know whether or not you are a connoisseur of wine. For if you have no feelings about wine one way or the other, you will want the sensation of drinking the stuff out of a vessel that may have cost thousands of pounds; but if you are a member of that vanishing tribe, the amateurs of fine vintages, you will choose the crystal, because everything about it is calculated to reveal rather than hide the beautiful thing which it was meant to contain.

With this paragraph Beatrice Warde begins her 1932 essay, 'The Crystal Goblet', which expands on the metaphor of the crystal goblet as the proper way to use typography: that the type and the page should be visually 'transparent', allowing one to read the text, uninterrupted by any other flavours or distractions from the type or its surround. But one only has to turn to the Japa-

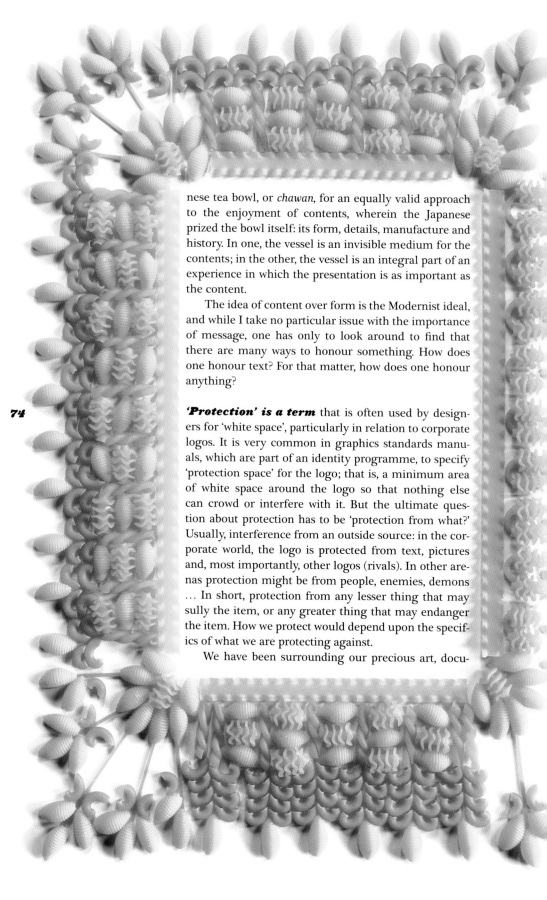

nese tea bowl, or *chawan*, for an equally valid approach to the enjoyment of contents, wherein the Japanese prized the bowl itself: its form, details, manufacture and history. In one, the vessel is an invisible medium for the contents; in the other, the vessel is an integral part of an experience in which the presentation is as important as the content.

The idea of content over form is the Modernist ideal, and while I take no particular issue with the importance of message, one has only to look around to find that there are many ways to honour something. How does one honour text? For that matter, how does one honour anything?

'Protection' is a term that is often used by designers for 'white space', particularly in relation to corporate logos. It is very common in graphics standards manuals, which are part of an identity programme, to specify 'protection space' for the logo; that is, a minimum area of white space around the logo so that nothing else can crowd or interfere with it. But the ultimate question about protection has to be 'protection from what?' Usually, interference from an outside source: in the corporate world, the logo is protected from text, pictures and, most importantly, other logos (rivals). In other arenas protection might be from people, enemies, demons … In short, protection from any lesser thing that may sully the item, or any greater thing that may endanger the item. How we protect would depend upon the specifics of what we are protecting against.

We have been surrounding our precious art, docu-

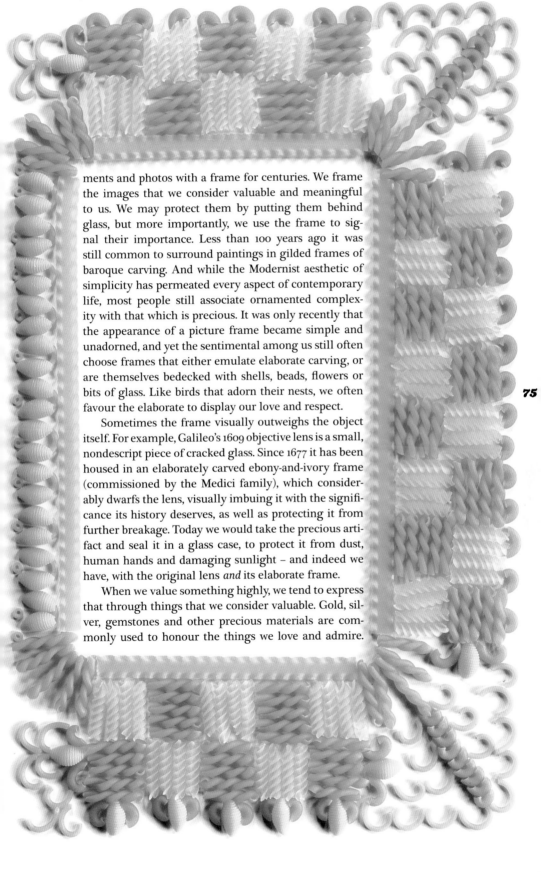

ments and photos with a frame for centuries. We frame the images that we consider valuable and meaningful to us. We may protect them by putting them behind glass, but more importantly, we use the frame to signal their importance. Less than 100 years ago it was still common to surround paintings in gilded frames of baroque carving. And while the Modernist aesthetic of simplicity has permeated every aspect of contemporary life, most people still associate ornamented complexity with that which is precious. It was only recently that the appearance of a picture frame became simple and unadorned, and yet the sentimental among us still often choose frames that either emulate elaborate carving, or are themselves bedecked with shells, beads, flowers or bits of glass. Like birds that adorn their nests, we often favour the elaborate to display our love and respect.

Sometimes the frame visually outweighs the object itself. For example, Galileo's 1609 objective lens is a small, nondescript piece of cracked glass. Since 1677 it has been housed in an elaborately carved ebony-and-ivory frame (commissioned by the Medici family), which considerably dwarfs the lens, visually imbuing it with the significance its history deserves, as well as protecting it from further breakage. Today we would take the precious artifact and seal it in a glass case, to protect it from dust, human hands and damaging sunlight – and indeed we have, with the original lens *and* its elaborate frame.

When we value something highly, we tend to express that through things that we consider valuable. Gold, silver, gemstones and other precious materials are commonly used to honour the things we love and admire.

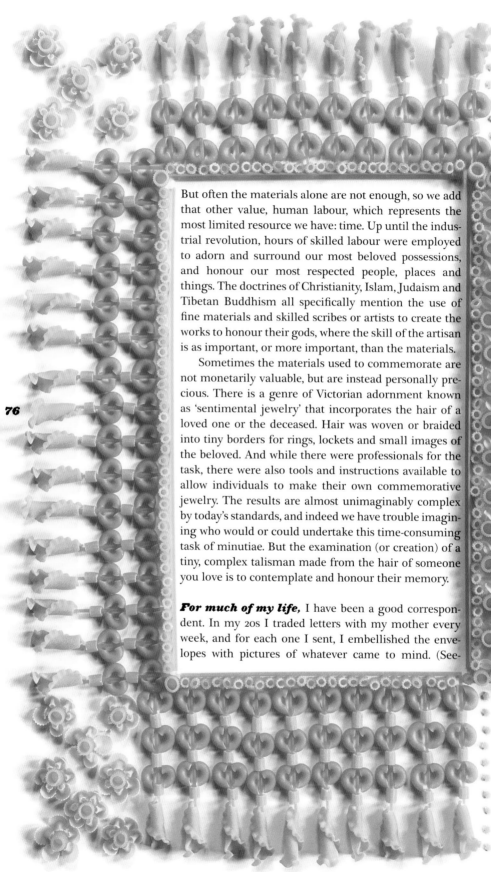

But often the materials alone are not enough, so we add that other value, human labour, which represents the most limited resource we have: time. Up until the industrial revolution, hours of skilled labour were employed to adorn and surround our most beloved possessions, and honour our most respected people, places and things. The doctrines of Christianity, Islam, Judaism and Tibetan Buddhism all specifically mention the use of fine materials and skilled scribes or artists to create the works to honour their gods, where the skill of the artisan is as important, or more important, than the materials.

Sometimes the materials used to commemorate are not monetarily valuable, but are instead personally precious. There is a genre of Victorian adornment known as 'sentimental jewelry' that incorporates the hair of a loved one or the deceased. Hair was woven or braided into tiny borders for rings, lockets and small images of the beloved. And while there were professionals for the task, there were also tools and instructions available to allow individuals to make their own commemorative jewelry. The results are almost unimaginably complex by today's standards, and indeed we have trouble imagining who would or could undertake this time-consuming task of minutiae. But the examination (or creation) of a tiny, complex talisman made from the hair of someone you love is to contemplate and honour their memory.

For much of my life, I have been a good correspondent. In my 20s I traded letters with my mother every week, and for each one I sent, I embellished the envelopes with pictures of whatever came to mind. (See-

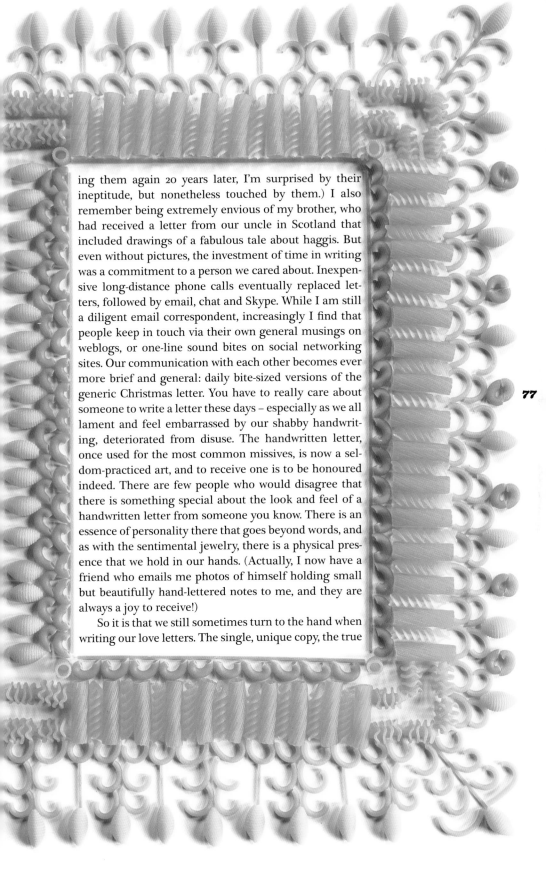

ing them again 20 years later, I'm surprised by their ineptitude, but nonetheless touched by them.) I also remember being extremely envious of my brother, who had received a letter from our uncle in Scotland that included drawings of a fabulous tale about haggis. But even without pictures, the investment of time in writing was a commitment to a person we cared about. Inexpensive long-distance phone calls eventually replaced letters, followed by email, chat and Skype. While I am still a diligent email correspondent, increasingly I find that people keep in touch via their own general musings on weblogs, or one-line sound bites on social networking sites. Our communication with each other becomes ever more brief and general: daily bite-sized versions of the generic Christmas letter. You have to really care about someone to write a letter these days – especially as we all lament and feel embarrassed by our shabby handwriting, deteriorated from disuse. The handwritten letter, once used for the most common missives, is now a seldom-practiced art, and to receive one is to be honoured indeed. There are few people who would disagree that there is something special about the look and feel of a handwritten letter from someone you know. There is an essence of personality there that goes beyond words, and as with the sentimental jewelry, there is a physical presence that we hold in our hands. (Actually, I now have a friend who emails me photos of himself holding small but beautifully hand-lettered notes to me, and they are always a joy to receive!)

So it is that we still sometimes turn to the hand when writing our love letters. The single, unique copy, the true

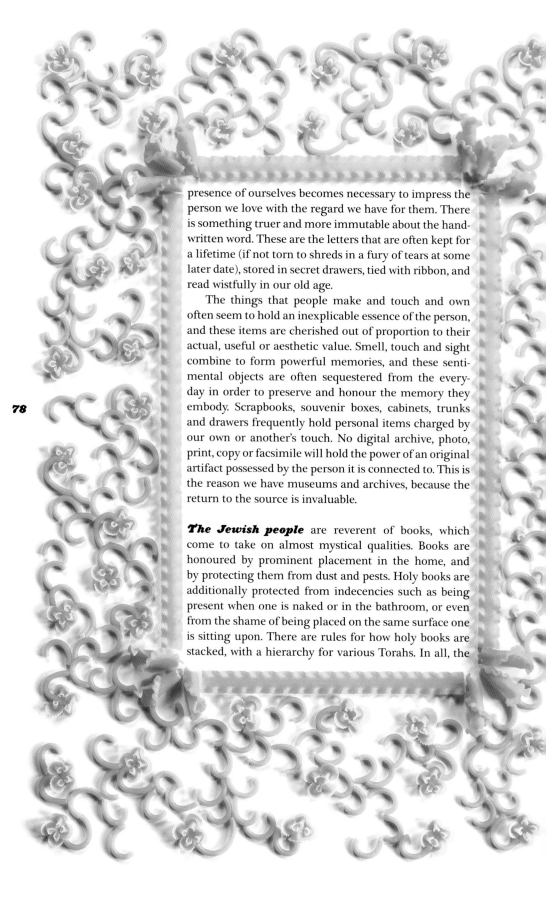

presence of ourselves becomes necessary to impress the person we love with the regard we have for them. There is something truer and more immutable about the hand-written word. These are the letters that are often kept for a lifetime (if not torn to shreds in a fury of tears at some later date), stored in secret drawers, tied with ribbon, and read wistfully in our old age.

The things that people make and touch and own often seem to hold an inexplicable essence of the person, and these items are cherished out of proportion to their actual, useful or aesthetic value. Smell, touch and sight combine to form powerful memories, and these senti-mental objects are often sequestered from the every-day in order to preserve and honour the memory they embody. Scrapbooks, souvenir boxes, cabinets, trunks and drawers frequently hold personal items charged by our own or another's touch. No digital archive, photo, print, copy or facsimile will hold the power of an original artifact possessed by the person it is connected to. This is the reason we have museums and archives, because the return to the source is invaluable.

The Jewish people are reverent of books, which come to take on almost mystical qualities. Books are honoured by prominent placement in the home, and by protecting them from dust and pests. Holy books are additionally protected from indecencies such as being present when one is naked or in the bathroom, or even from the shame of being placed on the same surface one is sitting upon. There are rules for how holy books are stacked, with a hierarchy for various Torahs. In all, the

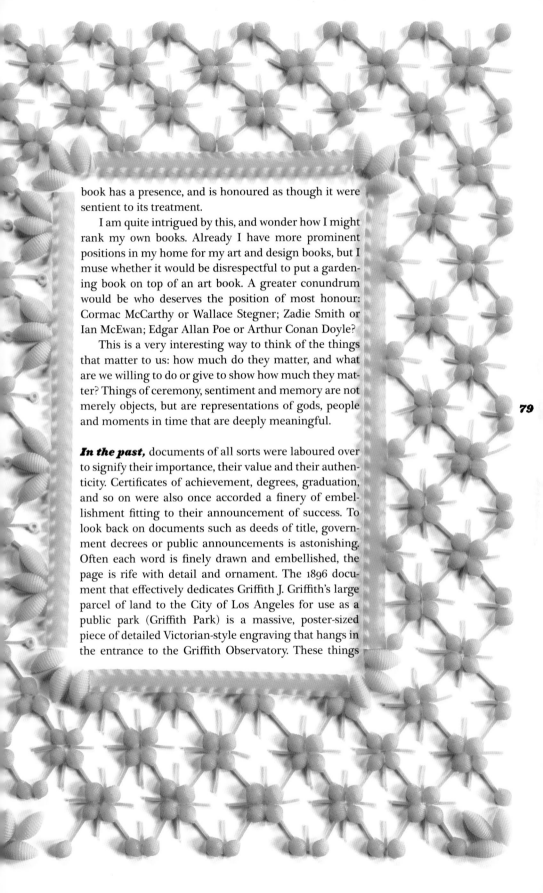

book has a presence, and is honoured as though it were sentient to its treatment.

I am quite intrigued by this, and wonder how I might rank my own books. Already I have more prominent positions in my home for my art and design books, but I muse whether it would be disrespectful to put a gardening book on top of an art book. A greater conundrum would be who deserves the position of most honour: Cormac McCarthy or Wallace Stegner; Zadie Smith or Ian McEwan; Edgar Allan Poe or Arthur Conan Doyle?

This is a very interesting way to think of the things that matter to us: how much do they matter, and what are we willing to do or give to show how much they matter? Things of ceremony, sentiment and memory are not merely objects, but are representations of gods, people and moments in time that are deeply meaningful.

In the past, documents of all sorts were laboured over to signify their importance, their value and their authenticity. Certificates of achievement, degrees, graduation, and so on were also once accorded a finery of embellishment fitting to their announcement of success. To look back on documents such as deeds of title, government decrees or public announcements is astonishing. Often each word is finely drawn and embellished, the page is rife with detail and ornament. The 1896 document that effectively dedicates Griffith J. Griffith's large parcel of land to the City of Los Angeles for use as a public park (Griffith Park) is a massive, poster-sized piece of detailed Victorian-style engraving that hangs in the entrance to the Griffith Observatory. These things

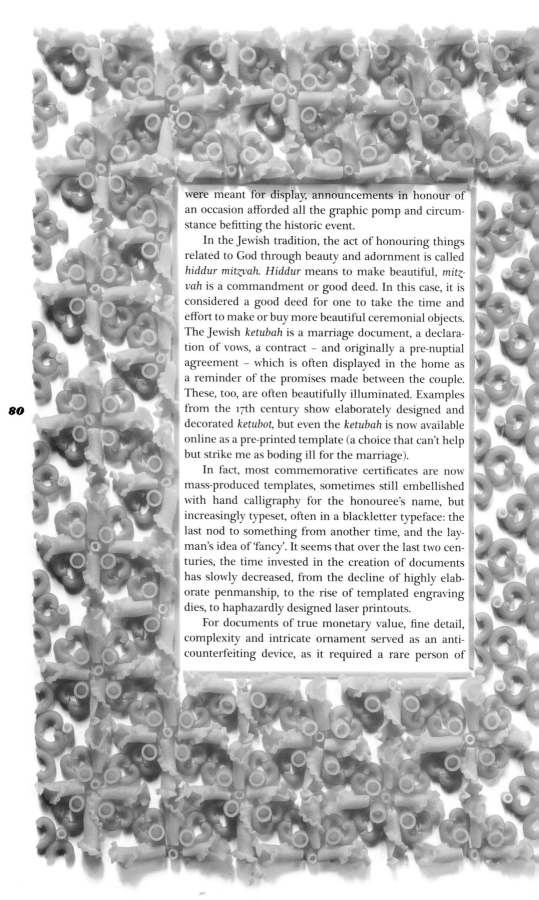

were meant for display, announcements in honour of an occasion afforded all the graphic pomp and circumstance befitting the historic event.

In the Jewish tradition, the act of honouring things related to God through beauty and adornment is called *hiddur mitzvah*. *Hiddur* means to make beautiful, *mitzvah* is a commandment or good deed. In this case, it is considered a good deed for one to take the time and effort to make or buy more beautiful ceremonial objects. The Jewish *ketubah* is a marriage document, a declaration of vows, a contract – and originally a pre-nuptial agreement – which is often displayed in the home as a reminder of the promises made between the couple. These, too, are often beautifully illuminated. Examples from the 17th century show elaborately designed and decorated *ketubot*, but even the *ketubah* is now available online as a pre-printed template (a choice that can't help but strike me as boding ill for the marriage).

In fact, most commemorative certificates are now mass-produced templates, sometimes still embellished with hand calligraphy for the honouree's name, but increasingly typeset, often in a blackletter typeface: the last nod to something from another time, and the layman's idea of 'fancy'. It seems that over the last two centuries, the time invested in the creation of documents has slowly decreased, from the decline of highly elaborate penmanship, to the rise of templated engraving dies, to haphazardly designed laser printouts.

For documents of true monetary value, fine detail, complexity and intricate ornament served as an anti-counterfeiting device, as it required a rare person of

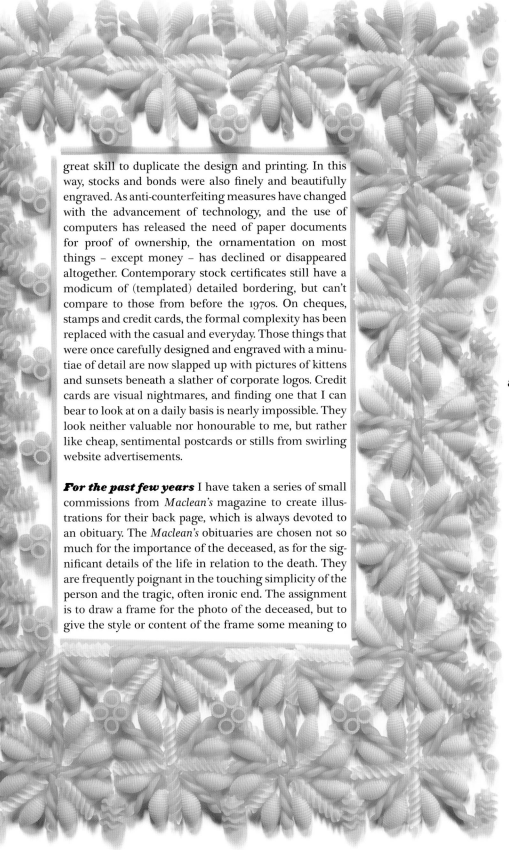

great skill to duplicate the design and printing. In this way, stocks and bonds were also finely and beautifully engraved. As anti-counterfeiting measures have changed with the advancement of technology, and the use of computers has released the need of paper documents for proof of ownership, the ornamentation on most things – except money – has declined or disappeared altogether. Contemporary stock certificates still have a modicum of (templated) detailed bordering, but can't compare to those from before the 1970s. On cheques, stamps and credit cards, the formal complexity has been replaced with the casual and everyday. Those things that were once carefully designed and engraved with a minutiae of detail are now slapped up with pictures of kittens and sunsets beneath a slather of corporate logos. Credit cards are visual nightmares, and finding one that I can bear to look at on a daily basis is nearly impossible. They look neither valuable nor honourable to me, but rather like cheap, sentimental postcards or stills from swirling website advertisements.

For the past few years I have taken a series of small commissions from *Maclean's* magazine to create illustrations for their back page, which is always devoted to an obituary. The *Maclean's* obituaries are chosen not so much for the importance of the deceased, as for the significant details of the life in relation to the death. They are frequently poignant in the touching simplicity of the person and the tragic, often ironic end. The assignment is to draw a frame for the photo of the deceased, but to give the style or content of the frame some meaning to

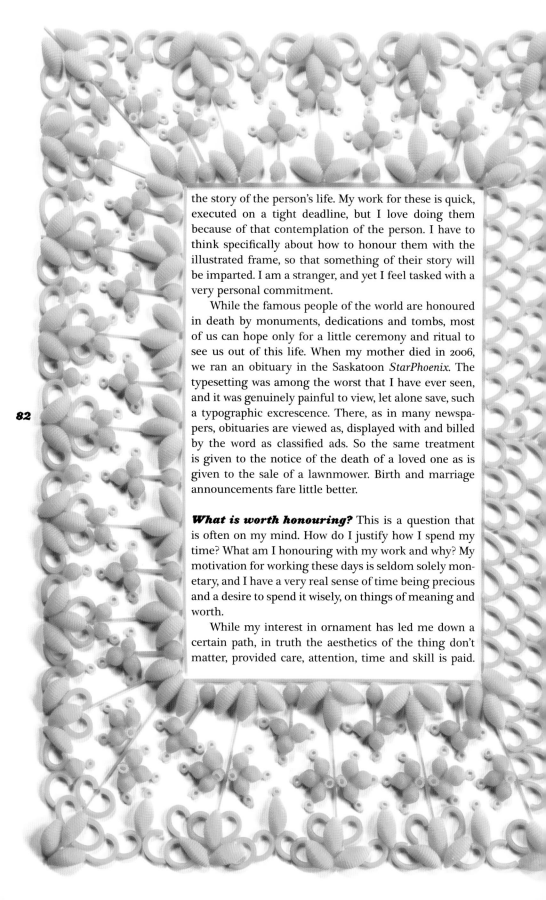

the story of the person's life. My work for these is quick, executed on a tight deadline, but I love doing them because of that contemplation of the person. I have to think specifically about how to honour them with the illustrated frame, so that something of their story will be imparted. I am a stranger, and yet I feel tasked with a very personal commitment.

While the famous people of the world are honoured in death by monuments, dedications and tombs, most of us can hope only for a little ceremony and ritual to see us out of this life. When my mother died in 2006, we ran an obituary in the Saskatoon *StarPhoenix*. The typesetting was among the worst that I have ever seen, and it was genuinely painful to view, let alone save, such a typographic excrescence. There, as in many newspapers, obituaries are viewed as, displayed with and billed by the word as classified ads. So the same treatment is given to the notice of the death of a loved one as is given to the sale of a lawnmower. Birth and marriage announcements fare little better.

What is worth honouring? This is a question that is often on my mind. How do I justify how I spend my time? What am I honouring with my work and why? My motivation for working these days is seldom solely monetary, and I have a very real sense of time being precious and a desire to spend it wisely, on things of meaning and worth.

While my interest in ornament has led me down a certain path, in truth the aesthetics of the thing don't matter, provided care, attention, time and skill is paid.

We all know when we have made an effort and when we have not; when we are compelled, and when not. I am respectful, and sometimes in awe of, the classically printed page, where text is king and all the details have been attended to. I am as moved by the perfection of a Modernist masterpiece as I am by a Baroque one. And I am equally touched by the inept but truly sincere attempt of a child or student. Sometimes the perfection is in the intent.

Many people are feeling bereft of meaning in their lives, and perhaps turn to religion to mark with ceremony the important passage of time, and to give a framework in which to celebrate life. But it's not necessary to worship in order to honour, and perhaps the void of meaning can be filled by paying closer attention to the things that matter. If we can identify what makes us happy, hopeful, respectful, or in some other way causes us to reflect, it's worthwhile to spend the time, effort and perhaps money to frame that thing, moment or experience with all the honour it deserves.

83

EMILY AVIGDOR
NÉE ... LOS...
AL...E
...ÉDÉE A PAR... L... 3 ...OVEMBR...
...GE... ... ANS

...e ARTHUR AVIGDOR
...ÉE MATHILDE CHAMBROV...
...ÉCÉDÉE LE 23 AOÛT 191...

RENÉ AVIGDOR
...IER DE LA ...GION D'HON...
...VIER 1867 – 7 ...ÉCEMBRE

ARTHUR J. AVIGDOR
...T 1840 – 16 FÉVRIER...

84

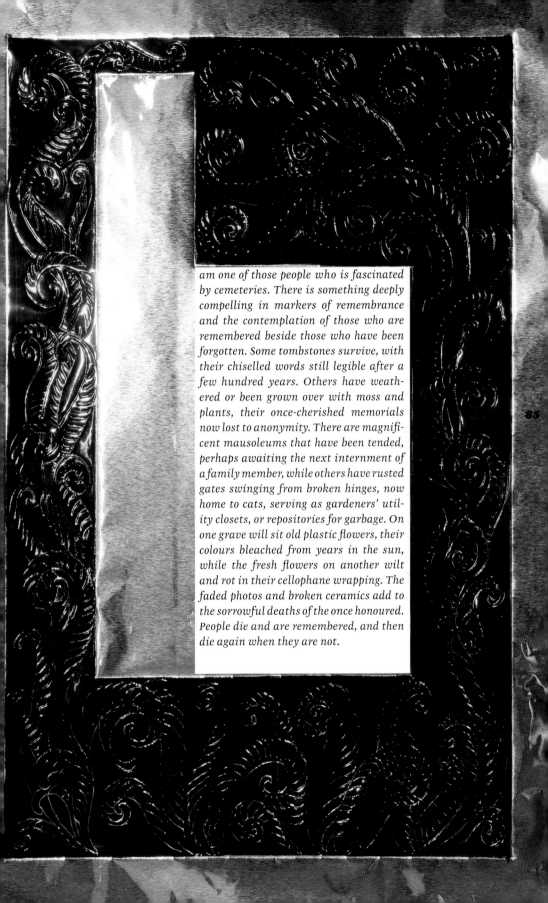

am one of those people who is fascinated by cemeteries. There is something deeply compelling in markers of remembrance and the contemplation of those who are remembered beside those who have been forgotten. Some tombstones survive, with their chiselled words still legible after a few hundred years. Others have weathered or been grown over with moss and plants, their once-cherished memorials now lost to anonymity. There are magnificent mausoleums that have been tended, perhaps awaiting the next internment of a family member, while others have rusted gates swinging from broken hinges, now home to cats, serving as gardeners' utility closets, or repositories for garbage. On one grave will sit old plastic flowers, their colours bleached from years in the sun, while the fresh flowers on another wilt and rot in their cellophane wrapping. The faded photos and broken ceramics add to the sorrowful deaths of the once honoured. People die and are remembered, and then die again when they are not.

88

93

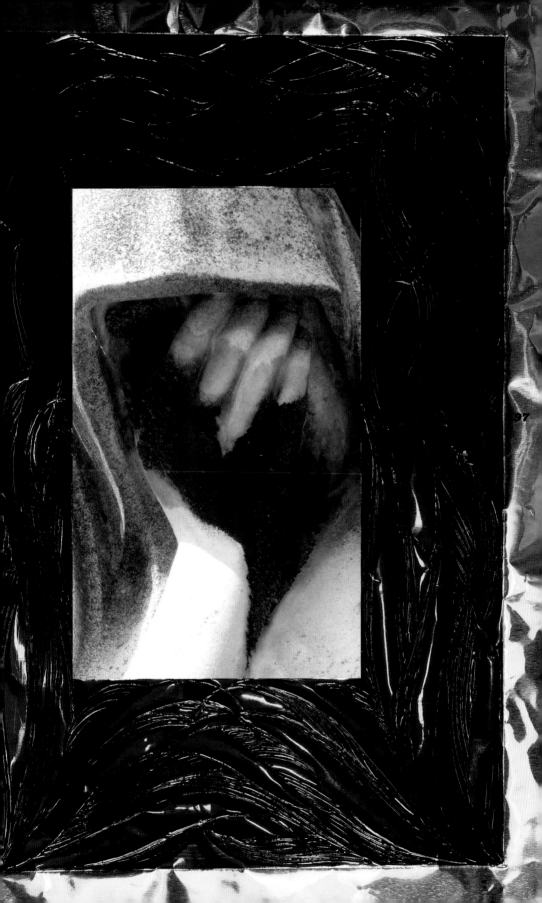

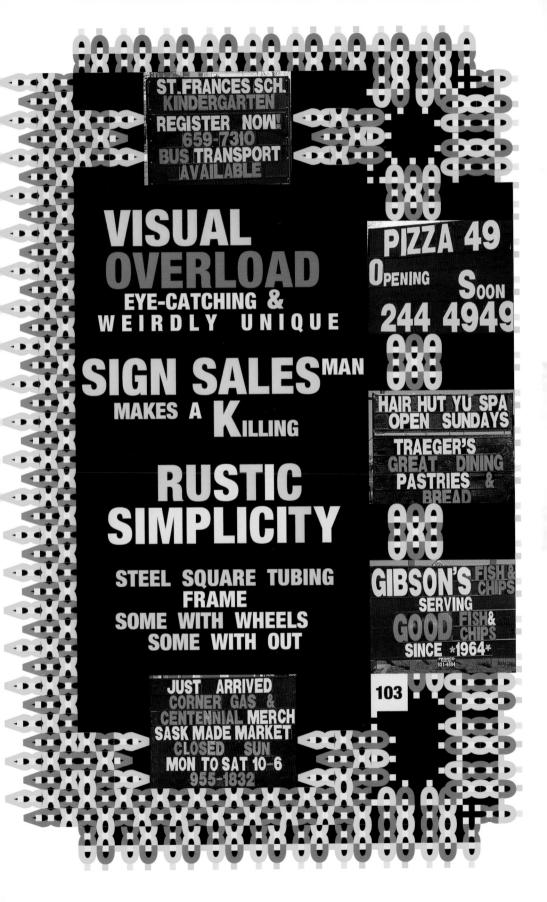

ST. FRANCES SCH.
KINDERGARTEN
REGISTER NOW
659-7310
BUS TRANSPORT
AVAILABLE

**VISUAL
OVERLOAD**
EYE-CATCHING &
WEIRDLY UNIQUE

SIGN SALESMAN
MAKES A **K**ILLING

**RUSTIC
SIMPLICITY**

STEEL SQUARE TUBING
FRAME
SOME WITH WHEELS
SOME WITH OUT

JUST ARRIVED
CORNER GAS &
CENTENNIAL MERCH
SASK MADE MARKET
CLOSED SUN
MON TO SAT 10-6
955-1832

PIZZA 49
OPENING SOON
244 4949

HAIR HUT YU SPA
OPEN SUNDAYS

TRAEGER'S
GREAT DINING
PASTRIES &
BREAD

GIBSON'S FISH &
CHIPS
SERVING
GOOD FISH &
CHIPS
SINCE *1964*
PENNCO
931-4594

103

LONEYS GOLF SHOP
SPRING GOLF SALE

SEW & HOME
NEW FURNITURE
COMING!
FLOOR MODELS
MUST GO!

BLOSSOMS
955-3355

SUMMER SALE
25-50% OFF
ENTIRE STOCK
PENNCO   931-4694

BEVERLY ASHDOWN
STUDIO 955-5400
SHOW YOUR LOVE
WITH A
MOTHER'S DAY
GIFT CERTIFICATE

104

PLYWOOD
PAINTED BLACK.
SOME PLASTIC STRIPS
TO   HOLD THE LETTE RS
& VOILA!

I BECAME OBSESSED.
DRIVING MY ELDERLY
MOTHER AROUND TOWN
I SLAM ON THE
BRAKES
CAREEN AROUND CORNERS
4 PHOTOGRAPHY

THANKS MUM!

TRAXX FOOT WEAR
OAKLEYS SUNGLASSES
NOW HERE

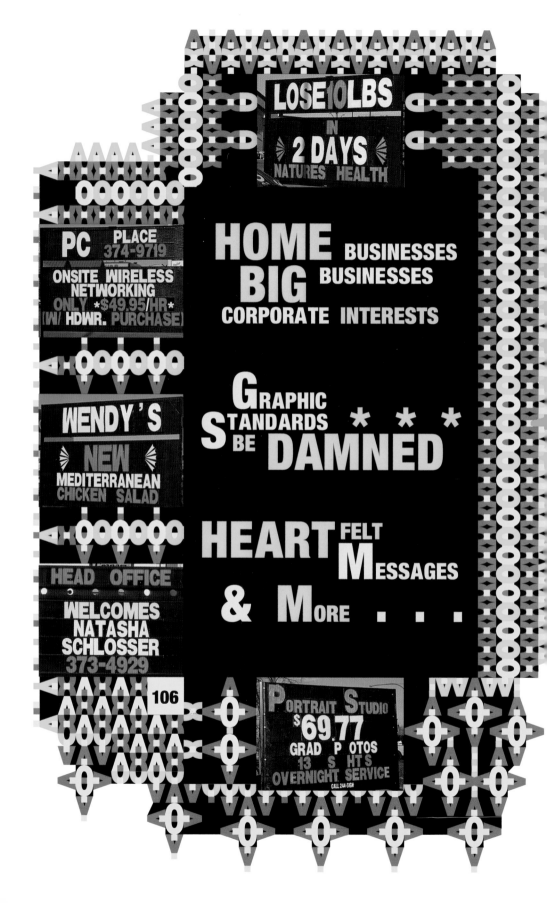

LOSE 10 LBS
IN
2 DAYS
NATURES HEALTH

PC PLACE
374-9719
ONSITE WIRELESS
NETWORKING
ONLY *$49.95/HR*
(W/ HDWR. PURCHASE)

WENDY'S
NEW
MEDITERRANEAN
CHICKEN SALAD

HEAD OFFICE
WELCOMES
NATASHA
SCHLOSSER
373-4929

HOME BUSINESSES
BIG BUSINESSES
CORPORATE INTERESTS

GRAPHIC
STANDARDS * * *
BE DAMNED

HEARTFELT
MESSAGES
& MORE ...

106

PORTRAIT STUDIO
$69.77
GRAD PHOTOS
13 SHTS
OVERNIGHT SERVICE
CALL 244-SIGN

CLOSING OUT
ALL
KIDS T SHIRTS .78 ADULT
DENIM JACKETS $14.98
ABBYS WAREHOUSE

VARIETY
OF EXPRESSION
IN A LIMITED RANGE

+

REMINISCENT OF EARLY
20TH C WOOD TYPE !

PERSONALITY TEST:
INVENTIVENESS
+ ACCIDENTAL 8RILLIANCE
OR SIMPLY ACCIDENCE

GARDEN BABIES
& KIDS
FRI&SAT
933-3393

MORTGAGE LINK
244-HOME
BUYING
OR
REFINANCING?
5YR   3.3%

WELCOME TO PETER D'S
OPEN FOR BREAKFAST
TRADITIONAL $4.99
SPECIAL
MO. LUNCH SPEC $8.99
STEAK SANDWICH
931-4894   PENNCO

SASKMADE
MARKETPLACE
SHOW YOUR
RIDER PRIDE
NEW ITEMS IN STORE
CALL 244-SIGN

109

COMPAQ ATHLON 64
3300+ COMPUTER
512M RAM 250 HD
DVDRW, 128VID XP
GRE T VALU $898

A PASSING PHASE
SOON TO B
REPLACD BY
A MORE 'SOPHISICATD'
VERSION OR DIGITAL
D1SPLAY

I WOULD LIKE TO
HAVE ONE IN
FRONT OF MY HOUSE
IT MIGHT SAY

GRAPHIC DESIGN
OR WHATEVER
WHILE U WAIT
* * * GRE T VALU * * *

E Z CASH
LOWEST CHEQUE
CASHING RATES
BRING IN YOUR
INCOME TAX
REFUND CHEQUES

CINDY MOLESKI
CUSTOM FRAMING
20% OFF
933-3393

3 OZ SPANAKOPITA
ON A BED OF RICE
W/ GREEK SALAD
& SM. POP $6.99

THE KEY TO
HEAVEN
WAS HUNG ON
A NAIL

111

SECRETS

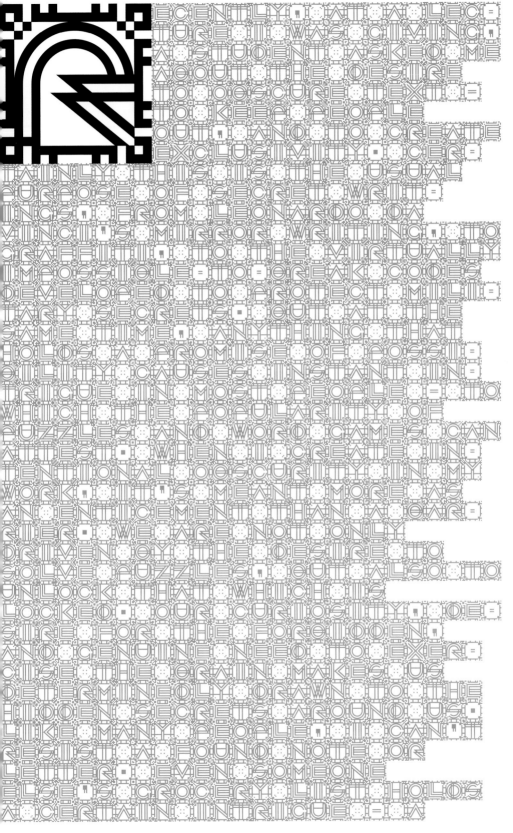

SCRAP OF A LIFE AN
OTHER PERSONS REALITY
AROUND WHICH BUILD MY
OWN IMAGINING OR CREATE A
STORY ONCE FOUND WILL
OFTEN SPEND CREATE EFFORT
OF OTHER CHAIN OF
ING AND LOOK FOR PERSONAL
CLUES THE MORE OBSCURE
HAS AN ACTUAL
INCREASINGLY RARE THE
QUEST OF ALL TWO
LIVES COLLIDE IN WRITING
AM THE INNOCENT
STANDER RECONSTRUCTING
MEANING FROM CLUES
ARE LEFT

EVEN OTHERS THAT I'VE
RECEIVED MYSELF LURED
BY THE WORDS OR PHRASES
THAT HAVE BEEN CROSSED
OUT AND WILL HOLD THEM UP
TO THE LIGHT OR EXAMINE
THE BACK TO TRY TO DECIPHER
WHAT TOUCH HAD ONCE
EXISTED THERE
COURSE SOMEONE ONCE
COMMUNICATE BUT
ANY ARCHIVING KNOWS OF THE
DELIGHT IN FINDING THESE
MISSING TOUCHES CHANCES
IN MUSIC NOTES AND
MARGINS IN BOOKS
WHAT WAS NOT SAID OR WRIT
TEN OR WHAT WAS NEVER
MEANT TO BE READ
MAKES US CURIOUS AND
INTENT

THE ALLURE OF SOMEONE
ELSE'S SOLITARY IS ALMOST

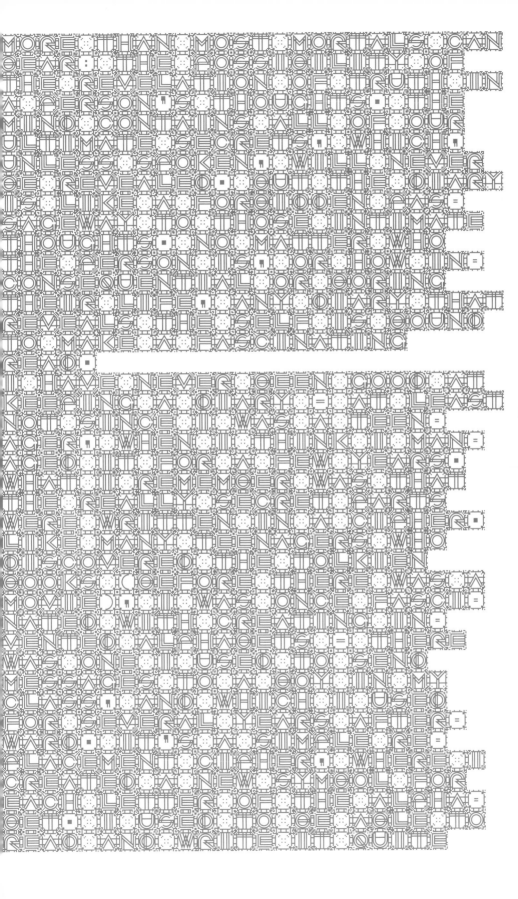

FLUENTLY AND EVEN AFTER
THIRTY FIVE YEARS I CAN
STILL REMEMBER A FEW
LETTERS.
OF COURSE THE VERY FACT
THAT SOMETHING IS EN-
CRYPTED HOLDS A PROMISE
FOR SOMETHING WORTH BREAK-
ING. IF WE WERE TO GO TO
TROUBLE OF BREAKING A
CODE TO A TEXT THAT
TURNED OUT TO BE MERELY
WHAT AUTHOR HAD FOR
BREAKFAST WE WOULD EITHER
BE VERY DISAPPOINTED OR
SUSPECT THE TEXT WAS
ITSELF A HERE CODE. SHE'S
MUCH SURELY OR EVEN MAD
OR THINGS POLITICALLY MUL-
LAYERED MEANING.
AS WITH ALL THINGS THAT
TAKE FOR GRANTED SHOULD
BE A REWARD WHAT COULD BE
WORTH THAN A LOVE LET-
TER EXCHANGE OF LOVE
LETTERS FROM THE VERY
BEGINNING OF A LONGING
A FAINT NEVER COME AND TO
BE READ AND WRITTEN IN
CODE.

116

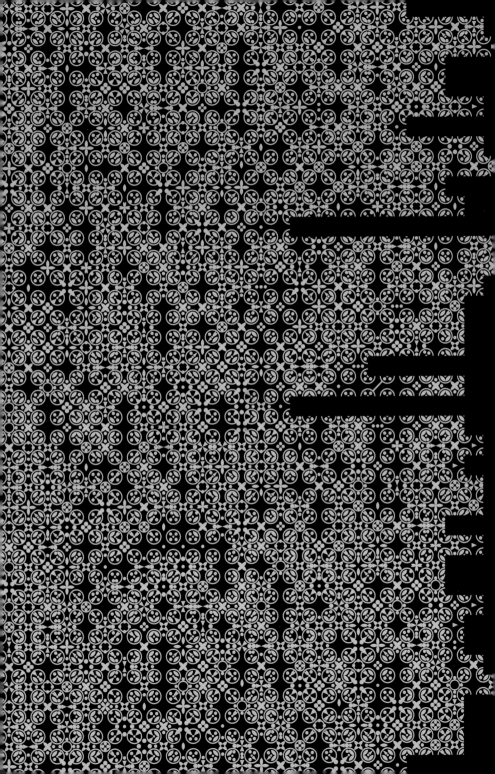

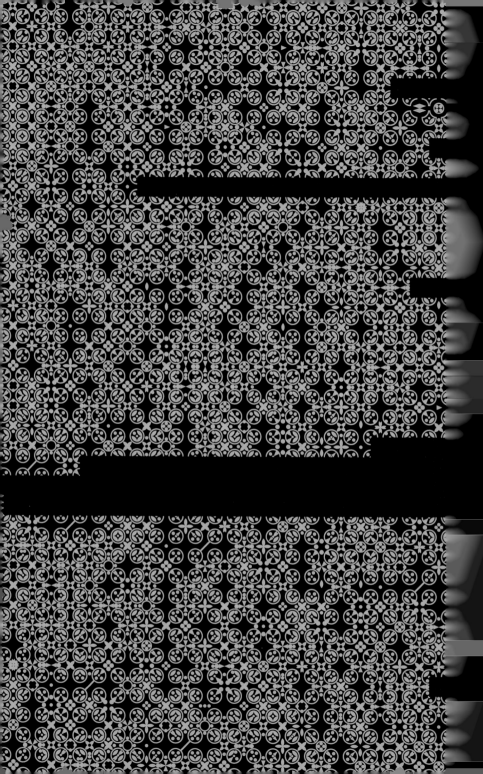

119

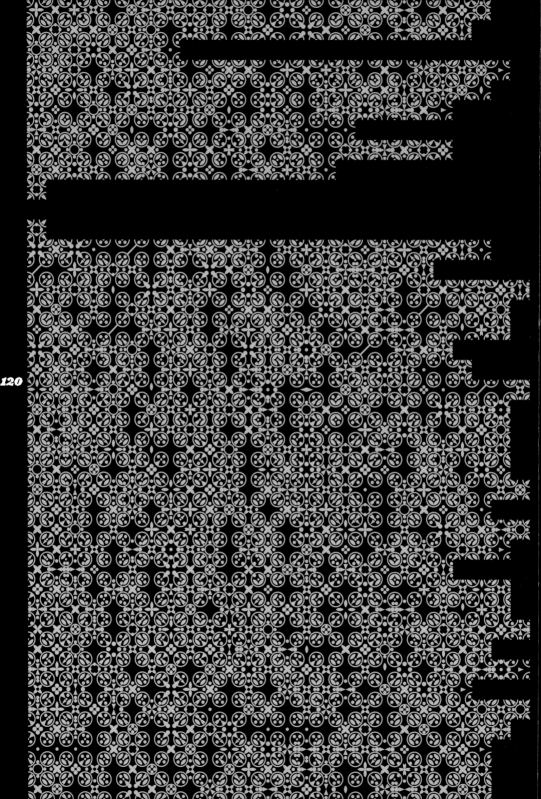

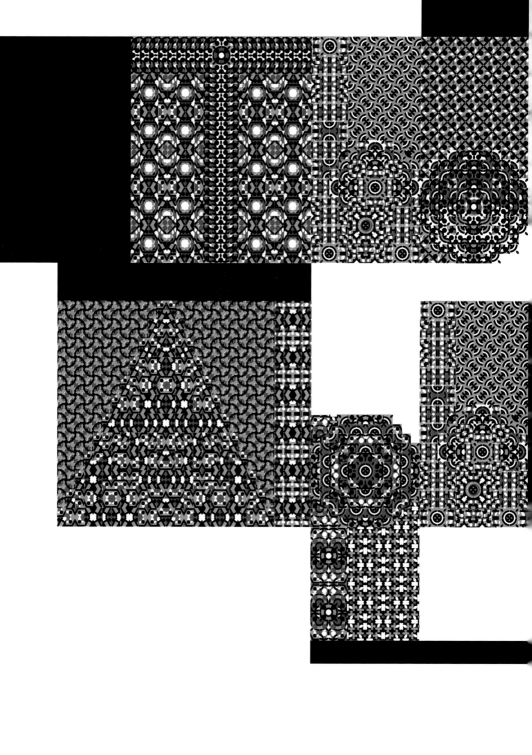

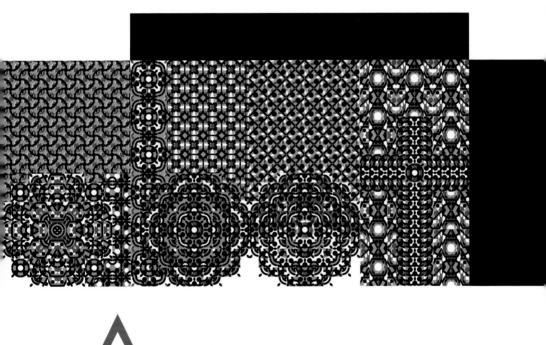

A
Critique

HAT ALPHABET

It's been around a long time, and I, for one, have some complaints. A lot of time has passed since this thing was so-called 'intelligently designed', in an age before we even knew there was such a thing as design. But we know more now, and, put to our current standards, it doesn't pass muster. I decided to give it a cold, hard look in the broad-spectrum light of the 21st century.

Aaa

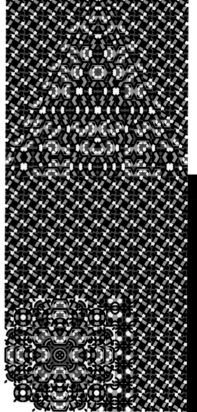

IT LOOKS like two different people designed this pair of letterforms, and they weren't talking to each other. The capital **A** has a good iconic structure: three strokes, and you're done. I like the way they lean together to form that stable triangular shape, both feet firmly on the ground, and the whole structure reinforced by the crossbar. It's very strong.

The lower-case **α** is just, uh … kind of stupid: a graphic non sequitur. But the double-storeyed form of the **a** has beautiful curves and allows for a lot of variation within the shape. It's feminine and extremely sexy, but sometimes the bowl causes problems. It has so little space to fit into: half the x-height! This is inconsistent with most other letters in the alphabet and seems a bit out of place. Neither is really working with that strong capital; I simply can't imagine what they were thinking.

Bb

THIS is a very nice pair. Whoever did this was really thinking about the relationship between the upper- and lower-case. I like the way the capital **B** has some variation in the proportions from top to bottom. It has muscle; it has fat.

Obviously designed by a man, the ball and stick of the lower-case **b** is simple and, appropriately, half of the capital **B**. Talk about male and female! That buxom, pregnant capital together with the excitable lower-case. *Bbbbeautiful.*

UNSUPERVISED junior designers. This is just lazy design, in my humble opinion. It is a curve, and a smaller curve. What's up with that? Think outside the circle.

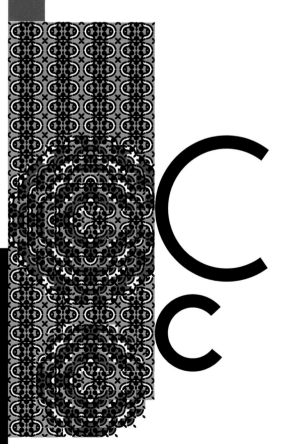

Cc

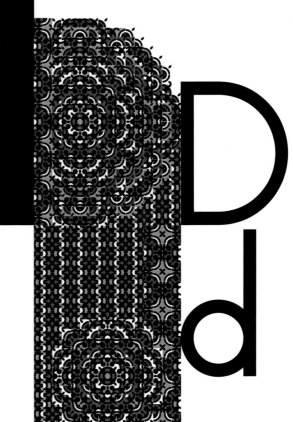

Dd

ANOTHER one from the scrapyard of design. The lower-case **d** is just a rip-off of the **b**, and it really bothers me how the capital **D** is flipped vertically. It's like someone wanted to emulate the **Bb**, but just didn't get it. This is not an ode, it's a poor derivative.

Ee

THESE may look like they don't belong together, but I think they're actually pretty good. The capital **E** has such good structure and balance, and in a way the lower-case **e** has that same structure, only rounded. One is based on a rectangle, the other on a circle. There's a concept behind this.

The eye of the lowercase **e** has some of the same problems as the **a**, though, due to that half-x-height thing. Would the capital **E** look better with another vertical line down the right? I think maybe it would. Something to think about.

127

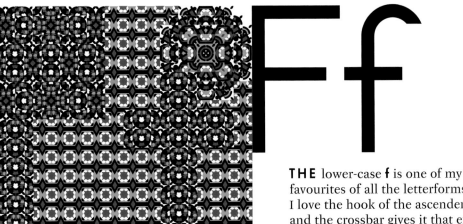

Ff

THE lower-case **f** is one of my favourites of all the letterforms. I love the hook of the ascender, and the crossbar gives it that extra oomph. But the capital **F**, although obviously related to the lower-case, is too close to the **E**. If the **E** had an extra stroke, then the **F** would stand out more. But still, it seems clumsy and top-heavy. I can see what they were trying to do by creating an angular version of the lower-case, I just don't think it's working.

Ggg

HERE we have two really great letterforms that just don't match! Perhaps designed by the same people who did the **Aaa**? Despite my problems with the **C**, I think the shape is expanded on in an inventive way in the **G**. Drawing an open lower-case **g** is one of the great pleasures in life – that beautiful curved descender! However, the two-storeyed form of the **g**, while quirky and amusing, is a baroque excess of unusual hooks and parts. It's incredibly difficult to remember what exactly goes where. In all, a litter of adorable mutts.

LIKE the **A**, the capital **H** is really strong. It has the same three parts as the **A**, and is clearly the work of the same designer. I like the balance of the open spaces top and bottom. The lower-case **h**, however, isn't doing anything for me. It looks weak and half-finished. I imagine it being the desperate result of a long night without ideas. It's the 'I just gotta make this deadline' solution.

THE capital **I** without the crossbars top and bottom is either the laziest piece of design in history or an elegant stroke of Modernism. With the crossbars, it's just clunky and awkward. The lower-case **i** is kind of cute with that little dot, I suppose, but I'm not really buying it. This one should have never made it out of the comp stage.

129

I HONESTLY think that a different designer saw the **i** and improved on it with the lower-case **j**. Where the **i** is boring and slightly weird, the addition of a swooping, curved descender turns it into a thing of beauty. The dot is now somehow emphatic, rather than silly. This one nailed it. The capital **J** was probably done afterward, borrowing the hook from the lower-case. But the top is problematic: without the crossbar it looks unbalanced; with it, it looks awkward. This is a design problem worthy of more thought.

JJj

SOMEONE had some fun with this one, and I like the results. An excellent pair. Both the upper- and lower-case **Kk** have character and – dare I say it? – attitude! It is very unique and balanced without resorting to the cliché of curves, and the flexibility of the joining of strokes allows for endless writing fun. A really excellent design.

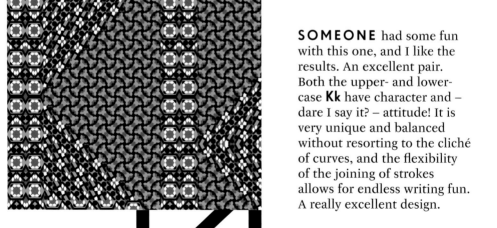

Kk

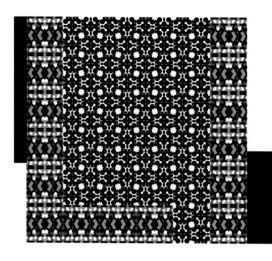

WHAT... the fuck ... is that? Surely no two worse letterforms exist than these duds – I mean, c'mon ... two lines and a line? Who designed this, some old fart completely worn out and bereft of ideas? The design rationale must've been one hell of a snow job. The capital **L** has that gaping, awkward open space, and the lower-case ... it's a line! And it looks like a capital **I** or a **1**, for God's sake. This is what happens when Modernism is allowed to run rampant. I'm so glad I don't have any of these in my name.

SPEAKING of my name, check these out. Now those are two sweet letterforms. Is it any wonder that a line of **m**s denotes 'yummy'? *Mmmm.* The capital **M** is unique and strong, balanced, and open in a way that doesn't interfere with other letterforms. The lower-case echoes the sturdiness of the capital, with all feet firmly on the ground, but with those two rolling curves. They both echo and embrace each other in well-deserved mutual admiration. *Yay!* My name begins with **M**!

Nn

WELL, it's half the **m**, and only half as nice. I do like the line per bend. Although it causes some directional problems when you're learning to write, it grows on you. The lower-case **n** is far less interesting. It looks lonely, missing its other half. The **Nn**s are amputees: fully capable of functioning, but just a little bit sad.

132

I DON'T know about this. At least they're not just straight lines, but they are, um ... just circles. There is beauty and perfection in a circle, but they're so self-enclosed, so unexpansive. I think they need something else ... like maybe a tail or something (see **Q**).

Pp

THE lower-case **p** is very nice, especially when you let the descender get really long, but this whole ball and stick thing ... c'mon guys, get over it! Given a choice, I prefer the **p** to the **b**, but the **b** did it first. That capital **P**, though, is just totally not working! Like a tiny girl with huge breasts, it's so top-heavy it looks like it's going to fall over! This whole letterform needs rethinking.

Qq

ALL the **O** really needed was a little something, and here it is in the capital **Q**. One of my all-time favourite letterforms, the **Q** takes all the beauty and simplicity of a circle and builds on it with the ever-variable and expressive tail: surely the chocolate cake of any type design. Too bad this letter is so seldom used.

The lower-case **q**, though ... I'm not fooled by that extra bit at the bottom of the descender – this is *another* ball-and-stick! The last one, I hope! This is no match for its elegant capital.

Rr

HERE, another pair where the upper- and lower-case have nothing in common, and must surely have been designed by two people. The capital is by a genius; the lower-case by a nincompoop.

The capital **R** takes the best from the **B** and the **K** and successfully merges them together. When the leg is not solidly, firmly, on the baseline, it is allowed to swoop below and become a tail – a form I particularly admire.

The lower-case **r**, on the other hand, is weak, imbalanced, stubby and awkward. It's an accursed thing that hangs around like a sick mongrel cur, drooling unpleasantly over all the other letterforms.

THIS was a great idea that lacks somehow in execution. Or rather, it's just really difficult to maintain a good standard. With all its potential for elegance, both the upper- and lower-case are hard to reproduce as anything other than clumsy and unbalanced by anyone other than trained experts. Try it, make me a good **S** ... it's hard! In the right hands, it's a sophisticated character, but horribly open to abuse – and certainly not something that should be entrusted to the hands of children. I also think the lower-case could benefit from a descender of some kind.

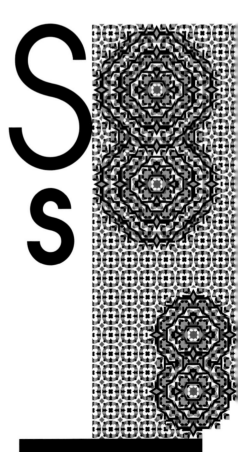

AFTER what I said about the L you might expect me to come down hard on the T, but where the capital L lacks balance, the T has it in spades. With its two arms, I find it welcoming and protective. Then move the arms down and shorten them and you've got a nice pair there! The lower-case minus the hook is a little bit Christian for my liking, though I do respect its simplicity. The hook gives it an interesting character, and I like it, despite being a tad unstable.

MY FIRST impression of this was that it was an obscenely lazy design: rocky, and derivative of the already poor Cc. However, after my initial outrage, I have come to recognize the anchoring aspect of the two straight sides of the U, and especially the firm little balanced foot of the lower-case u. Suddenly I am drawn to their tongue-like nature and the crystal goblet form.

Vv

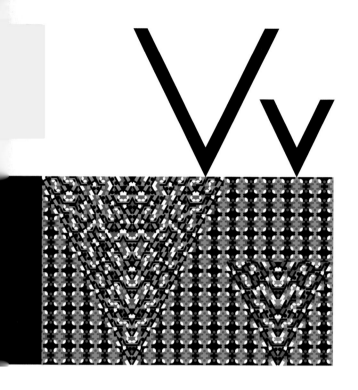

THE V has a split personality. On the one hand, it's so unstable, balancing on that point like a cheeky upside-down **A**, but on the other, it has a certain confident pride. Both arms raised equally above the nadir, it manages to instill a trust that it will not actually fall over, despite the precariousness of the situation. And it's just a nice form. Maybe I'm partial to triangles.

The shrunken lower-case **v** obviously gets my scorn – it's like telling a good story twice in a row.

Ww

THE exuberance of the **V** translates twofold to the **W**. But where the **V** teeters, the **W** stands solid. The **W** has the symmetry and pleasing balance of the **M**, without being a directly inverted version of same. I like it when the strokes cross in the middle too. But is it because we are nearing the end of the alphabet that we see this endless repetition of shrunken lower-case forms? Do I hear, 'Fuck it, we're nearly done. Let's just get this job outta here'?

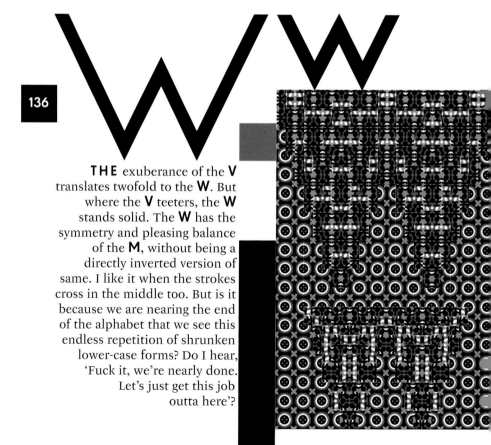

X

x

DID Paul Rand design this? Is it not perfect? Do you know why illiterates sign their name with an **X**? Because it's perfect, that's why. Two strokes, which give the illusion of four.

Personally, I would have turned it 45 degrees for the lower-case, but hey, you don't argue with Mr Rand.

Xxxx, you know I love you.

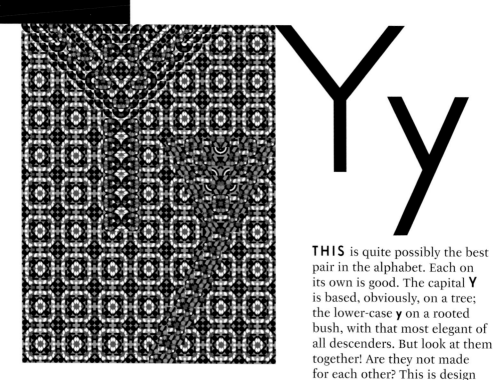

Yy

THIS is quite possibly the best pair in the alphabet. Each on its own is good. The capital **Y** is based, obviously, on a tree; the lower-case **y** on a rooted bush, with that most elegant of all descenders. But look at them together! Are they not made for each other? This is design that thinks and understands relationships. I guess it to be the later work of the designer of the **Bb** and the **Mm**.

AND last, but certainly not least, the **Z** – with a final flourish, a sword slash (yes, I know!), a signature of completion. The **Z** has both action and balance – the zeal of a project at its end! Alas, with the lower-case **z**, the alphabet goes out with a bang *and* a whimper.

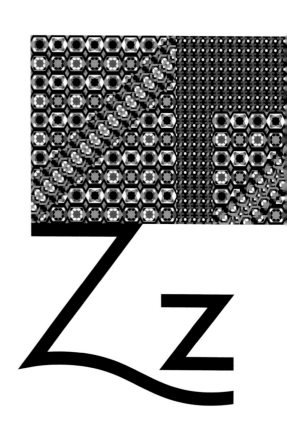

Zz

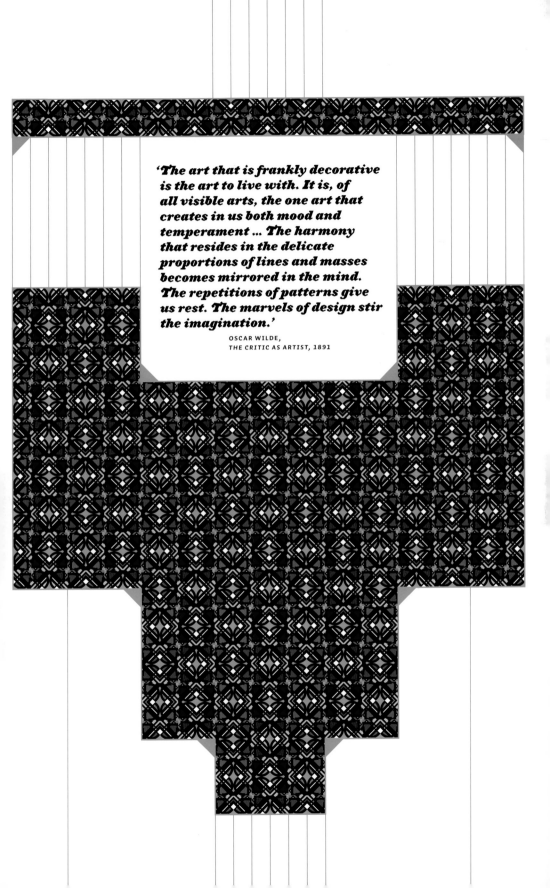

'The art that is frankly decorative is the art to live with. It is, of all visible arts, the one art that creates in us both mood and temperament ... The harmony that resides in the delicate proportions of lines and masses becomes mirrored in the mind. The repetitions of patterns give us rest. The marvels of design stir the imagination.'

OSCAR WILDE,
THE CRITIC AS ARTIST, 1891

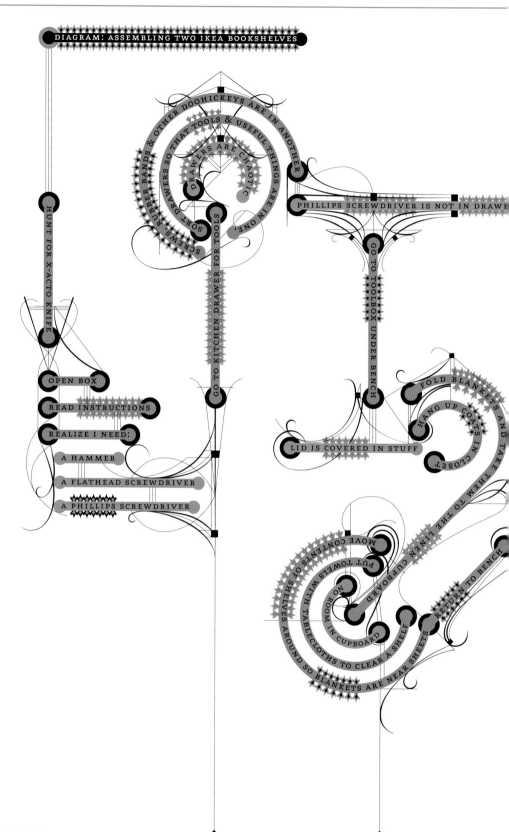

DIAGRAM: ASSEMBLING TWO IKEA BOOKSHELVES

HUNT FOR X-ACTO KNIFE

SORT DRAWERS SO THAT TOOLS & USEFULTHINGS ARE IN ANOTHER

SCREWS, RUBBER BANDS, & OTHER DOOHICKEYS ARE IN ANOTHER

DRAWERS ARE CHAOTIC

PHILLIPS SCREWDRIVER IS NOT IN DRAWER

GO TO KITCHEN DRAWER FOR TOOLS

GO TO TOOLBOX UNDER BENCH

OPEN BOX

READ INSTRUCTIONS

REALIZE I NEED:

A HAMMER

A FLATHEAD SCREWDRIVER

A PHILLIPS SCREWDRIVER

LID IS COVERED IN STUFF

FOLD BLANKETS AND TABLE

HANG UP COATS IN CLOSET

MOVE CONTENTS OF

PUT TOWELS WITH

THEM TO THE LINEN CUPBOARD

PUT TOWELS WITH

NO ROOM IN CUPBOARD

RETURN TO BENCH

TABLECLOTHS TO CLEAR A SHELF

SHELVES AROUND SO BLANKETS ARE NEAR SHEETS

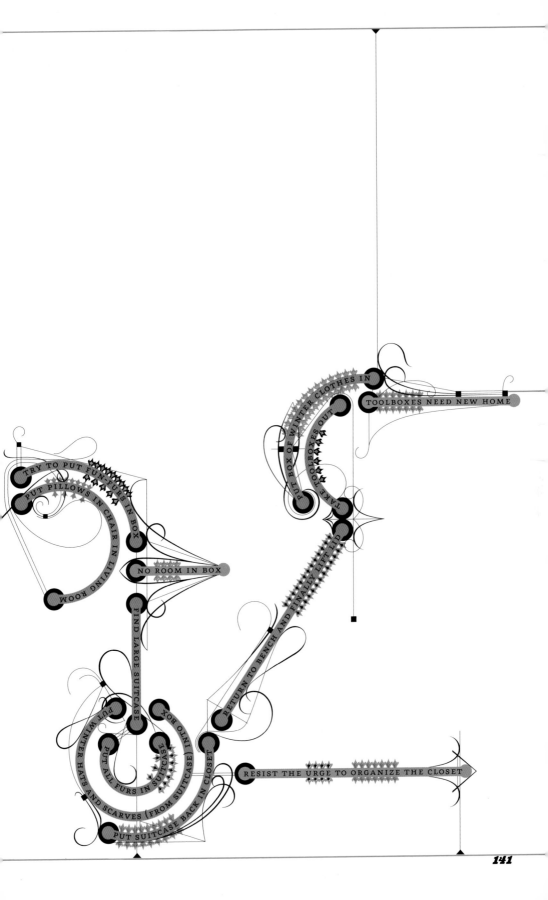

TRY TO PUT FUN FURS IN BOX

PUT PILLOWS IN CHAIR IN LIVING ROOM

PUT BOX OF WINTER CLOTHES IN

TAKE TOOLBOXES OUT

TOOLBOXES NEED NEW HOME

FINALLY LIFT LID

NO ROOM IN BOX

FIND LARGE SUITCASE

RETURN TO BENCH AND

PUT WINTER HATS AND SCARVES (FROM SUITCASE

PUT ALL FURS IN SUITCASE

PUT INTO BOX

PUT SUITCASE BACK IN CLOSET

RESIST THE URGE TO ORGANIZE THE CLOSET

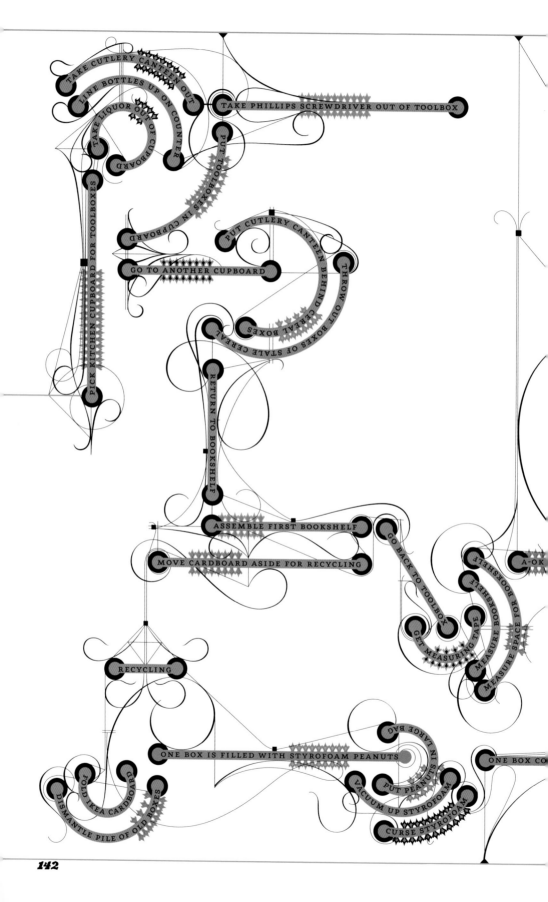

TAKE CUTLERY CANTEEN OUT
LINE BOTTLES UP ON COUNTER
TAKE LIQUOR OUT OF CUPBOARD
TAKE PHILLIPS SCREWDRIVER OUT OF TOOLBOX
PUT TOOLBOXES IN CUPBOARD
PICK KITCHEN CUPBOARD FOR TOOLBOXES
PUT CUTLERY CANTEEN BEHIND CEREAL BOXES
GO TO ANOTHER CUPBOARD
THROW OUT BOXES OF STALE CEREAL
RETURN TO BOOKSHELF
ASSEMBLE FIRST BOOKSHELF
GO BACK TO TOOLBOX
A-OK
MOVE CARDBOARD ASIDE FOR RECYCLING
GET MEASURING TAPE
MEASURE BOOKSHELF
MEASURE SPACE FOR BOOKSHELF
RECYCLING
PUT PEANUTS IN LARGE BAG
ONE BOX IS FILLED WITH STYROFOAM PEANUTS
ONE BOX CO
FOLD IKEA CARDBOARD
DISMANTLE PILE OF OLD BOXES
VACUUM UP STYROFOAM
CURSE STYROFOAM

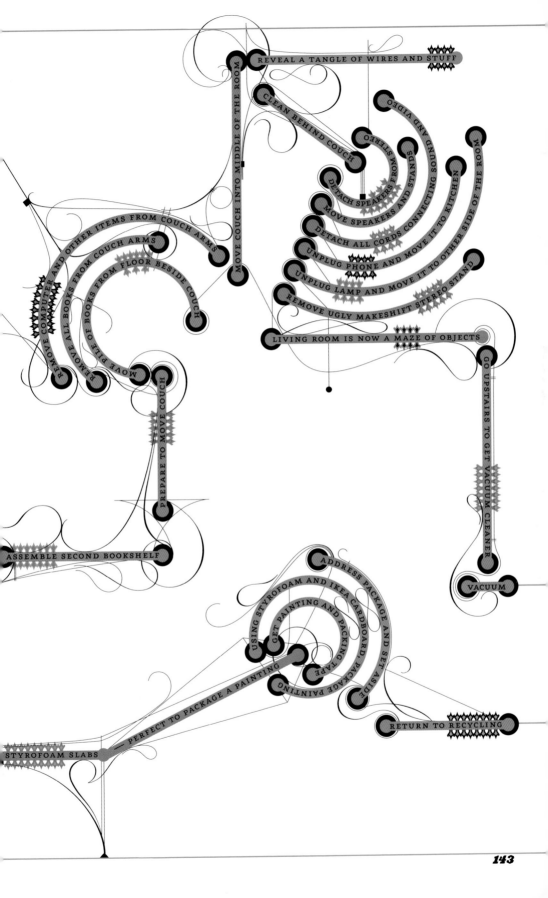

REVEAL A TANGLE OF WIRES AND STUFF

CLEAN BEHIND COUCH

MOVE COUCH INTO MIDDLE OF THE ROOM

SOUND AND VIDEO

DETACH SPEAKERS FROM STEREO AND STANDS

MOVE SPEAKERS AND STANDS

DETACH ALL CORDS CONNECTING SOUND

UNPLUG PHONE AND MOVE IT TO KITCHEN

UNPLUG LAMP AND MOVE IT TO OTHER SIDE OF THE ROOM

REMOVE UGLY MAKESHIFT STEREO STAND

REMOVE COMPUTER AND OTHER ITEMS FROM COUCH ARMS

REMOVE ALL BOOKS FROM COUCH ARMS

REVEAL PILE OF BOOKS FROM FLOOR BESIDE COUCH

MOVE PILE OF BOOKS

LIVING ROOM IS NOW A MAZE OF OBJECTS

GO UPSTAIRS TO GET VACUUM CLEANER

PREPARE TO MOVE COUCH

ASSEMBLE SECOND BOOKSHELF

VACUUM

ADDRESS PACKAGE AND SET ASIDE

GET PAINTING AND PACKAGE PAINTING

USING STYROFOAM AND IKEA CARDBOARD, PACKAGE PAINTING

PERFECT TO PACKAGE A PAINTING

RETURN TO RECYCLING

STYROFOAM SLABS

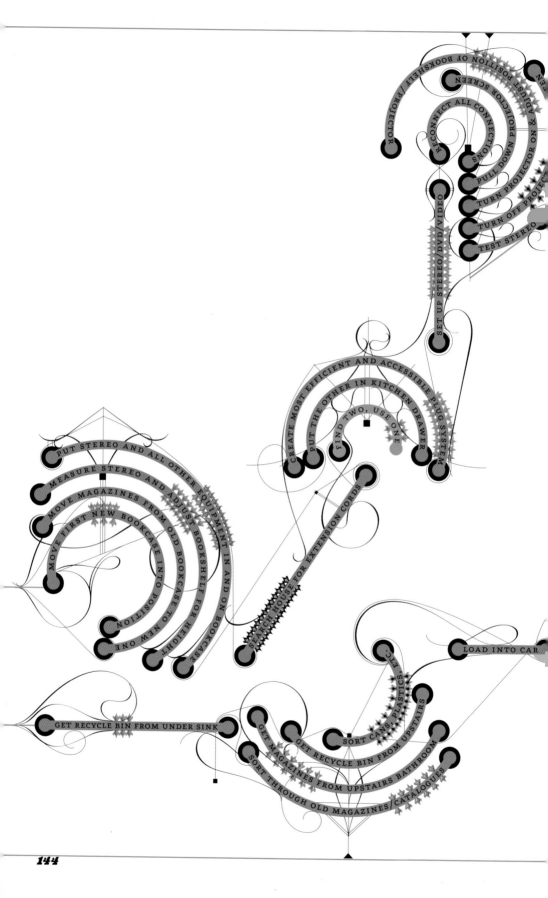

ADJUST POSITION OF BOOKSHELF/PROJECTOR SCREEN

RECONNECT ALL CONNECTIONS

PULL DOWN PROJECTOR SCREEN

TURN PROJECTOR ON

TURN OFF PROJECTOR

TEST STEREO

SET UP STEREO/DVD/VIDEO

CREATE MOST EFFICIENT AND ACCESSIBLE PLUG SYSTEM

PUT THE OTHER IN KITCHEN DRAWER

FIND TWO, USE ONE

PUT STEREO AND ALL OTHER EQUIPMENT IN AND ON BOOKCASE

MEASURE STEREO AND ADJUST BOOKSHELF FOR HEIGHT

MOVE MAGAZINES FROM OLD BOOKCASE TO NEW ONE

MOVE FIRST NEW BOOKCASE INTO POSITION

SEARCH HOUSE FOR EXTENSION CORDS

LOAD INTO CAR

GET RECYCLE BIN FROM UNDER SINK

SORT CANS, PLASTICS, ETC.

GET RECYCLE BIN FROM UPSTAIRS

GET MAGAZINES FROM UPSTAIRS BATHROOM

SORT THROUGH OLD MAGAZINES/CATALOGUES

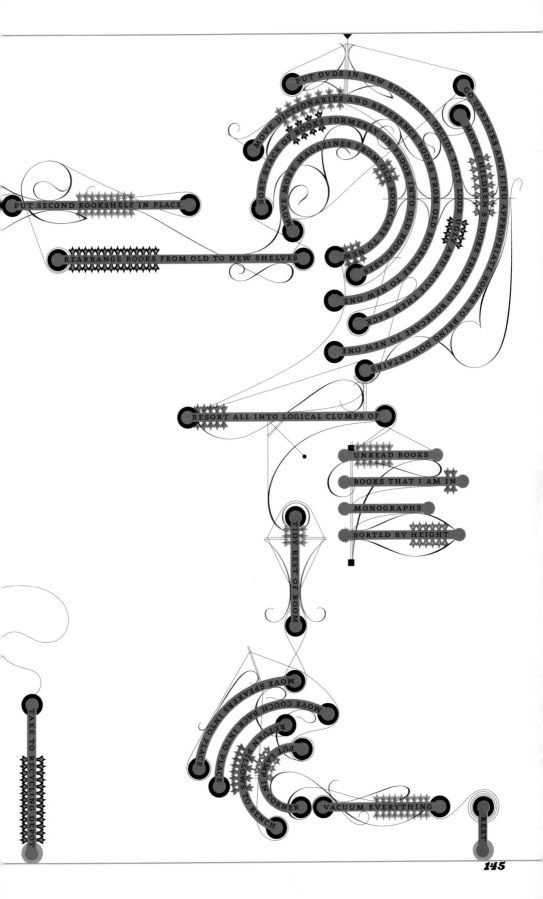

PUT DVDS IN NEW BOOKCASE

MOVE DICTIONARIES AND REFERENCE BOOKS

DECIDE THEY LOOK UGLY AND MOVE THEM BACK

GO UPSTAIRS AND FIND APPROPRIATE BOOKS FROM OLD BOOKCASE TO NEW ONE

SORT STACK OF BOOKS FORMERLY ON FLOOR INTO OLD BOOKCASE

MOVE CHILDREN'S BOOKS FROM OLD BOOKCASE TO BRING DOWNSTAIRS

MOVE MORE MAGAZINES FROM OLD BOOKCASE TO NEW

MOVE MAGAZINES FROM OLD BOOKCASE TO NEW ONE

PUT SECOND BOOKSHELF IN PLACE

REARRANGE BOOKS FROM OLD TO NEW SHELVES

RESORT ALL INTO LOGICAL CLUMPS OF

UNREAD BOOKS

BOOKS THAT I AM IN

MONOGRAPHS

SORTED BY HEIGHT

TIDY REST OF ROOM

MOVE SPEAKERS

MOVE COUCH BACK INTO PLACE

RETURN PILLOWS

PUT LAMP IN CORNER

PUT BLANKET ON BENCH

VACUUM EVERYTHING

TAKE TO RECYCLING DEPOT

REST

Marian Grade 1

MEMORY

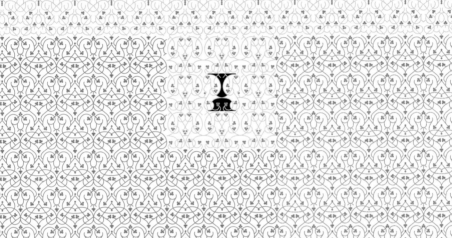

I

PHOTO-

GRAPHY

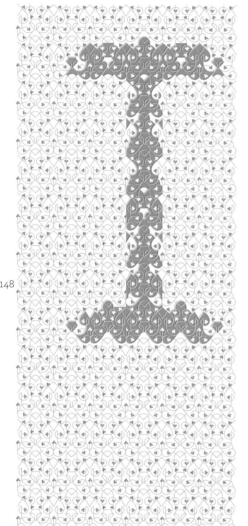

People, lost and found

am not a person who likes to collect, partly because of my obsessive tendencies and my fear that once I indulge in a penchant for buttons, teacups, or whatever else strikes my fancy, I'll become overwhelmed and my house will fill up with useless things. For this reason, I tend to avoid garage sales and dubious roadside 'antiques' shops. But when I do allow myself to be drawn in, the one thing I can never resist are old photographs. I'm not terribly interested in the quality, or in determining historical value. In fact, the less I know of the people I find, the better, and the age of the photo is only important in that it's apparent that time has passed, that the person in the photo will have undoubtedly changed, might be old, or long dead. I look at these photos of a moment captured by one person who cared about the other, who has or had a life, and I wonder, who were they, what were they thinking in that moment, and what happened to them? I contemplate the person, and they are alive to me.

A number of years ago, at a garage sale in my home town of Saskatoon, I came across a box of framed 8×10 photos of two little boys, taken over a period of a few years. When I took them out of their frames, written on the backs of each were their names: Ronnie and Sheldy. I guess they were taken in the 1950s, and that Ronnie and Sheldy are probably still alive, a little older than me. But here in these photos, they are two little boys, and as such they will always remain to me. I took them home and kept them – I still have them – and in a sense I adopted Ronnie and Sheldy into my own memory. I don't make up stories about them, or think about them much at all, except that Ronnie and Sheldy were found in a box, and they now belong to me.

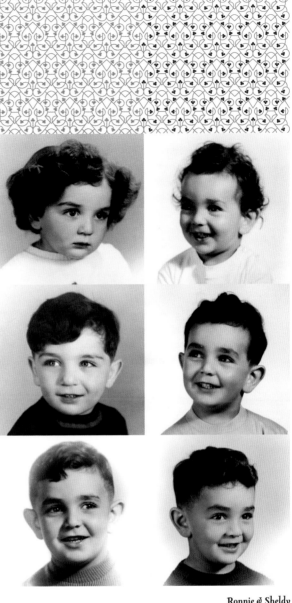

Ronnie & Sheldy

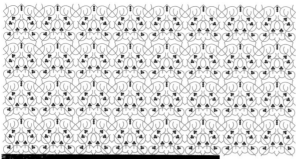

Mud Family

One of my favourite finds is a photo that I uncovered from a pile of soaking wet leaves in the gutter in Vancouver. There were other photos in the street that day, and I regret not taking them as well, but this one is a prize. It shows what I assume is a family of six, in the woods, completely naked, with their bodies slathered in drying mud. They look happy and proud of themselves, and I can imagine what a terrific day it was for them and how each of them must hold this moment clearly in their memory – only I have the photo. Being naked, outside, covered in mud is not completely foreign to my own family, and there is something about the photo that looks like the 1970s to me, although there's nothing to identify an era, and with this photo I feel as though I might have been there. Where I adopted Ronnie and Sheldy, in a way I feel that this family adopted me. If I were to lose this photo, in some strange way I would be as upset as – perhaps even more than – if I had lost one of my own family photos. To me, this photo is my key to a collective memory of another family, like a doorway into a different universe.

I do wonder, though, how photos get discarded this way. People move, things disappear, get lost and then found again; sometimes people purposely discard their possessions and their memories; and, of course, they die, and their possessions change from meaningful to garbage. This is perhaps what interests me most:

that change from being one who is loved to one who is discarded. My ex-husband confessed that he lost many things that were once ours, including photos, so I too have been discarded in some form. Perhaps someone found and has a photo of me on the day of my wedding – myself wearing one of the strangest outfits (a man's coat and tails with patterned Indonesian pants), with the odd, ragtag group of four people in Jericho Park, Vancouver – and wonders who I am. Perhaps I am taped to a computer monitor: an adopted sister of an unknown person.

The archival artifact and the significance of the historical edit

When my mother died, I was given the task of sorting, repairing and rebuilding our family photo albums. I found myself faced not only with a monumental task, but a variety of moral and historical/archival conundrums. The albums stop and start. Some have only a few photos (like the one that my grandmother started, which pathetically contains only a handful of photos of my mother up to age 5, but in and of itself is significant for that fact), some are well organized and cohesive, and some contain fading scraps of newspaper and magazine clippings along with the photos. One of the reasons I am meant to sort and rebuild the albums is that some of them are in a terrible state of decay. Pages and photos are bent, torn, falling out and missing. Photos of uncertain date and place float, unanchored, while blank spots gape, with names written under them.

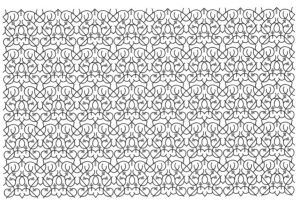

The expert

My mother, June Bantjes, in 1954.

Repair is possible, but the paper is not archival – it's very weak and prone to further tearing and damage.

One of the albums in worst condition is the one from Mum's young adulthood. But as I contemplated dismantling it, I was stopped by my mother's handwriting around each photo. Not only is her handwriting extremely precious to me, but it is part of the memory artifact. The album itself is a piece of her life, and it seems wrong to dismantle it, even though it's damaged and will only get more damaged. In addition to the nostalgia of her handwriting, her commentary on the photos is touchingly personal. Under one of the photos of herself on the beach wearing a snorkle and mask, she has written, 'The expert.' Clearly written jokingly, this has such a strong invocation of the moment. It is the type of thing that a young person writes very close to the time of the event: allusive, playful, and somehow full of memory. But the memory that it's full of is my mother's, and she is dead. So for me, it triggers an imagination of her memory, much in the same way I imagine the memory of the unknown naked mud family. (Nor was she without a sense of humour. Above the photo of my first day at school she has written, 'Shades of the prison house.')

As I look through my mother's albums, once I

Marraine with Lord Lauderdle & Mr Scott (!)

My great-grandmother stands with two people who have absolutely no connection to my family.

get past family, which is of immediate interest to me, I encounter photos of people and places that were of significance to her, but are completely unknown to me or anyone else left in the family. They were preserved and cherished by my mother, but in a sense they died with her. They were someone she knew, and now they are nobody in the context of my family history.

The captions contain alluring details. My great-grandmother Marraine stands with Lord Lauderdale (who, with a bit of research I now know is Ian Maitland, 15th Earl of Lauderdale) and a 'Mr Scott'. Who is Mr Scott, and why does he deserve an exclamation mark after his name? Where photos are missing, the caption remains as a key to the imagination of the photo. I know what Marraine looks like, so I then conjure up an image of her in Pretoria.

With each subsequent rebuilding of family histories, stray characters in the story are often erased, ending up in garage sales or fluttering down the street. They get culled from the single-minded focus of the family. Which leads me to wonder,

1950.
Marraine in Pretoria

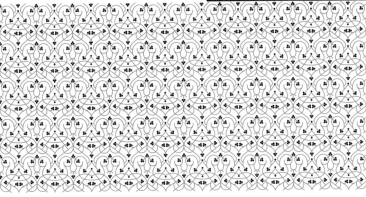

Colin & Angela

what is the purpose of a family photo album? Is it the last remaining document of my mother's memory? If so, for that sake these strangers should remain a part of our family history. If the photo albums weren't damaged, I would certainly leave everything intact: my mother's handwriting tells the story; the people remain anchored in the places and time of her life. But what is the point of having an artifact so delicate it can no longer be perused without fear of disintegration?

If I rebuild the albums, everything changes. If I create something new with my own handwriting in place of my mother's, I destroy one piece of personal history while creating another. It is a very appealing idea to make something that creates a continuous history with all of the collected material in such a way that we and our future family can look at it and it feels relevant. If I am creating a new history, a family history that includes my mother, when I come to the photos of these mysterious personal appendages, I don't know what to do. If I throw them out, what am I dismantling? If I keep them, what are they?

The wealth and variety of potential information

In the collection of family photos, there are also pictures that are loose, framed, and multiples where some are exact duplicates of the one in the album, while others are slightly different shots. The latter are particularly interesting in that they fill in gaps and provide a

touch of movement, like frames from a film: alternate realities to the ones that become fixed in our memory via a single photo image. We've all had the experience of taking several shots of a person, and while none of them are ideal as a single photo, the collection tells so much more about that moment in time: the way she turned her head; how she looked sad one second and laughed the next; how the two of them look at each other in that one frame out of many. To find the out-takes many years later is twice as fascinating: memory, once static, is renewed. But it causes even more indeci-sion for the archival process.

I have also discovered multiples and out-takes in negatives that my father sent me a few years ago. On scanning the negs, I discovered another variable in the process: colour. The scanned negatives were much richer in colour, and with a broader spectrum, than the prints. In essence, they were more 'true', but the prints have the appearance of 'authenticity' in that they have a particular colour that I associate with that time, and with my memory of the photos themselves. I found myself with another conundrum: to adjust the colour of the digital file to match the print, or not?

So what does one do with all these copies? Choose the best and leave the rest on the street for some curi-ous person like myself to find? Or do I archive them in boxes and envelopes, as has been done in the past? If these were historically significant, obviously one would catalogue and save, but for a personal history, while alternate photos of my mother are significant to me, they will be increasingly insignificant to my

Marjorie Muir & June Bantjes, 1995

brother's children and, later, their children. Ultimately they will be tossed away, so why not toss them now?

Divergent histories

Taking all of the above into account, once we hit the '70s all hell breaks loose, as Mum essentially stopped keeping a proper photo album, despite her best intentions. As we kids grew older and acquired friends and eventually our own lives, our own histories diverged from our mother's. In her collection are not only photos of our friends, spouses, ex-spouses, etc., but also of her own friends and their children.

So now that I am entering the area of construction, rather than preservation or reconstruction, do I attempt to construct the history of Mum's life? Do I try to tell her story, guessing at the time, significance and identity of people I barely knew, yet who I know were significant to her? Or do I just toss bits of her history into the garbage, and create my own memory of her, making the photo album either my memory of her life or some kind of simulacrum of a family history, from my perspective?

Additionally, there is the problem of my father, who was divorced from my mother in 1965. He has his own photo albums, but I have copies of some of his photos in my collection. Am I compiling a history of my mother's life, or the family's? If the latter, I should mix some of my dad's photos into the timeline. But what about photos of Dad with old girlfriends, or in places

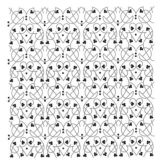

where we were not? How do I – or do I – mix these divergent histories in with my mother's? I feel like I'm organizing a seating arrangement for an elaborate party of the dead. Who should be invited, and who not? Who should sit next to whom?

Constructive power

Much of this is about speaking for the dead to the unborn, or the unknown. It's about selectively writing history, and recreating the past from a future perspective. We think of documented histories as fixed in place. We imagine them to have more permanence than stories and oral histories. But time wears out media and materials, so disintegration and reconstruction are inevitable, and each time it's done there is interpretation, which puts incredible power in the hands of the interpreter: in this case, me.

My father, Dennis Bantjes, and – ?

157

With the construction of my family's historical record in photos, I'm looking backward and attempting to choose the select moments that will fix our history, quite possibly for all time. From my omniscient present I have the power to obscure the more painful moments and erase the mundane, if I so choose.

As in Rufus Wainwright's song, 'Damned Ladies', where he calls out warnings to the singers in the opera, I observe this history of my mother, and wish that I could warn (or comfort) her of what lies ahead. How happy she looks here, how unhappy there. I want to tell her to do this, not that, or assure her that it will all work

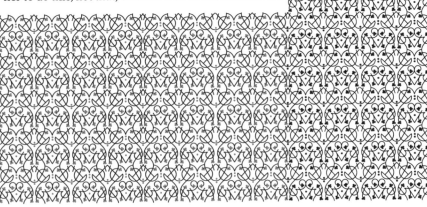

Mum, 1960.

out in the end. Then I look at my own photos from my own life, and want to tell myself the same.

With my power of hindsight, I have the potential of not reconstructing a history, but of creating a fiction based on a desired quasi-history. If I erase the trail of the original documents, my construction will become family fact. The mischief-maker in me is tempted to include some red herrings.

In 2008 I was in one of the many street markets in Berlin, perusing old photos, when I discovered an interesting trend. I was intrigued by the old-looking photo albums that were not nearly worn enough to have actually seen much use, but that frequently contained full collections of photos of Nazi war officers. None of them had captions, and the photos were all suspiciously intact. On closer inspection I realized that there were seldom re-occurring individuals, and I concluded that these were albums assembled by contemporary dealers from a plethora of discarded old photos (one can only imagine how many people jettisoned the Nazis from their family history), without regard to who or what was in them. In fact, it was likely that most of these people had never known each other, and here they were, sharing this space side by side as though they had once been family, friends or comrades. Their association now is not that they were once members of the same army, but that they were once members of the same defiled regime over which a fetishistic fascination has evolved, to the extent that there is a market to support collecting them together as strangers,

completely devoid of history or personality. The small irony in that is not lost.

Reconstructive power

The other power I have, which exists outside of the privacy of my family albums, is to resurrect the dead and give them new life in a new setting: for instance, here in this book. Ronnie and Sheldy were discarded, then they became my adopted photos for about 20 years, and now they exist here, with new life, and certainly you will look at them and think about them. They will remain here, and have renewed but ever-changing significance to many unknown people until this book is no longer in use, and the last remaining copy disintegrates into dust. But until then, I have extended their lives by many, many years. I'm bursting with the power of it!

159

With the photos of my mother, I have also extended her life – and although to you she is more mutable and abstract than she is to me, she retains a link to her actual history through me (which Ronnie and Sheldy do not). I am the author whose words you are reading, and she is my actual mother.

I first discovered this amazing power that I, as a designer and producer of mass-printed things, have, when I made a poster for the paper company Stora Enso on 'Sustainability'. (In the spirit of all things mutable, Stora Enso no longer exists, having been bought by another company shortly after the posters were made.) I was thinking about history and families and generations, and I wanted to invoke that in the

Unknown German soldiers from a Berlin flea-market.

poster through archival images – some from the public domain, and some from my own archives. And it was part way through this process that I realized what I was doing: that I was taking images of these people, printing them in a new context, and sending them into new environments. There, people would look at them and wonder. Perhaps some of them would look familiar, and perhaps some people would even form a small bond with one or more of them. Further, they are strangers assembled together at a party. They come from different times and places, but together they now represent a continuum of humanity.

I have no idea who this is.

Exerting my power once again, one of the images I used in the poster is from a photo I bought in a store in Saskatoon. I don't know who he is, or when it was taken, but he looks a bit like an old friend of mine, as though he could have been her great-uncle. And now he alone of all the people I used in my poster has been given yet another life.

Is this disrespectful? I don't think so. It could be, if I resurrected someone to represent a potentially objectionable idea, or to use them as an unflattering example. But I see this more in the line of my adoption of Ronnie and Sheldy. Sometimes images of meaning are discarded, and sometimes images of no meaning are adopted and given new life.

My brothers and I, Christmas.
My mother with me.
A house.

The meaning of that image will change over time and from person to person, but such is the way of all things.

The transformation of the everyday

My favourite images from our family collection are those taken in the '50s and '60s with a Kodak Brownie camera. The photos are, I believe, typical of photos taken by the slightly inept, amateur documentarists of the time: crooked landscapes with heads of children sliding out of the frame, wildly off-centre portraits, blurry images and a lot of sky and ground. Thousands of photos of people standing, casually facing the camera, fully aware of its presence but not as stiff and formal as the professional plate cameras of half a century previous. Nor do they share the candid, tell-all air of the Polaroid (though they are similar in shape and size). They are intentionally, but inexpertly, composed. They are one's family, but they could be anyone's family. Accidentally, they are strangely 'arty'.

Even with negatives, these pictures are practically impossible to enlarge. There is a softness to the images that

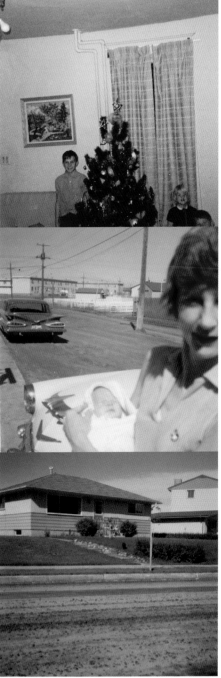

My brother Michael with my mother, 1969. Below, painting of same.

will never surrender more detail. A few years ago I began to make paintings of some of my favourites of the family photos. I had intended to do many, but never got past three. Still, the process was interesting. Starting with something that was personal and mundane, I elevated it to something that was more personal, in that I had made it, and 'art', which is usually, by intention, public. If I were a better painter, and more dedicated to what I started, I could imagine the series making an interesting exhibit. It was a celebration of the universality of the everyday. Those snapshot moments catapulted from the personal photo album to the gallery walls would have triggered the memory of each viewer's own snapshots, ricocheting back to their photo albums resting at home.

The eternal march of technological advance

Meanwhile, as my endless waffling over the scraps of photographic paper continues, the documentation of my own history is now entirely digital. My photos, from approximately 2003 onwards, are not albums or stacks of unsorted prints, but thousands of digital files of various quality and in various sizes and formats. I have begun sorting them, weeding the good shots from the bad, collecting by year, and naming them something indicative of their content and time. My intent was to print them out, and add them to the other paper pho-

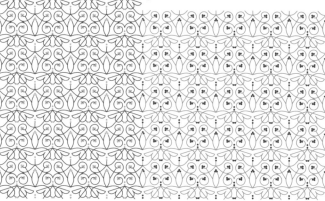

tographs. But ... is that backwards? Perhaps I should be scanning the older photographs and creating digital albums. I've considered getting a digital photo frame, and running them in continuous loop. Is that what people do now? Is that what they'll do in the future? I'm convinced that at some point one of these formats – paper or digital – will become cumbersome to me, but which one is anybody's guess.

Not having children, I feel I have only myself to worry about, though it's possible that my niece or nephew will inherit this task. Perhaps they will come to me in 20 years and record me into some kind of box. I'll hold up old photos of myself, my brothers, my mother, and tell old-lady stories in my creaky voice. Perhaps I'll include Ronnie and Sheldy, or the naked family, spin false memories of the wonderful times we had together, and it will all be preserved in the box until that, too, is discarded by people who no longer care.

Memory is what keeps us in place, in time. But our ability to shape and construct the past takes many forms, and those who take it on have great power in what we project to the future. Images of people are always so compelling for what we recognize and what we seek to recognize. They're so much more than an image of a thing or a place because we're able to project ourselves and our understanding of what it is to be human into them. When we look at a picture of someone and think about them as a person, we bring them to life. This is perhaps the closest to immortality that we will ever get.

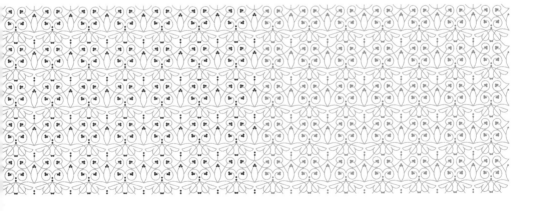

hether or not you believe in Santa Claus, or even have him as part of your culture, chances are high that you recognize the Santa icon, despite an extremely broad range of visual interpretation. Santa is a symbol of Commercial Christmas, and although the mythology surrounding him varies from country to country, in North America this icon is fairly fixed within a set of graphic parameters. This makes him instantly identifiable within a wide variety of alternatives (whereas the Easter Bunny has almost no distinguishing characteristics, and God could just as easily be any eccentric old man).

I'm interested in how the Santa identity is maintained, and what it is exactly that makes Santa, Santa.

At its most complete, the Santa set is comprised of a fat, older white man, with a white beard and moustache, a red outfit and pointed, floppy hat trimmed with white fur and a pom-pom, a wide black belt, boots, mittens, and assorted paraphernalia and hangers-on (sleigh, elves, reindeer, bells, sack, etc.). This image is attributed in part to the 19th-century illustrator Thomas Nast, who was the first to use red and white for the outfit. It was also famously adopted and promoted by the CocaCola company in the 1930s.

The ingredients are sufficient enough to ensure that the Santa icon can appear in any number of forms or media without loss of recognition. From ceramics to felt to knitwear, you name it, Santa's been made from it. But it's also incredibly flexible, to the

extent that almost any of the characteristics can be swapped, altered or removed, and it still remains recognizably Santa. Let's start with that suit.

The Santa on the left is a kind of ersatz ur–Santa. Any robed Santa is a reference to his origins as St Nicholas, depicted in bishop's robes, but we are unconfused. The length or volume of drapery in the costume is immaterial, provided it isn't gathered like a dress. However, the addition of stars or other embroidery does push the boundaries of the costume to the extreme. Starred robes evoke wizards, and the fellow on the left is decidedly Gandalfian, while the one below him seems to have been bred from a yak. The question is: if this were July would we still recognize these figures as Santa? I say, yes. In combination with the other attributes (notably the long, pointed hat and white beard), the fact that the robes are red is a dead giveaway.

So is the colour red a requirement for the icon Santa?

Not necessarily. Blue, green: still Santa. White, or no colour at all: still Santa.

And of course, the popular Chocolate Santa – robed or unrobed, delicious.

How about facial features? Beyond the beard, what constants are required for this icon to remain Santa? None. Santa is not a character. Although traditionally fat, he can be emaciated, have giant tumours for cheeks or have, essentially, no features at all and still be recognizable at fifty paces. There are black Santas, which I find fully believable, so I would posit that skin colour does not matter either.

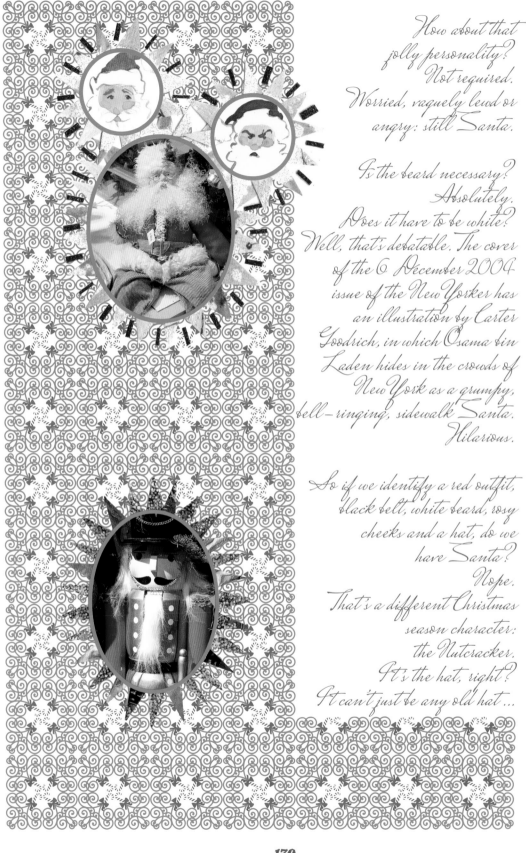

How about that jolly personality? Not required. Worried, vaguely lewd or angry: still Santa.

Is the beard necessary? Absolutely. Does it have to be white? Well, that's debatable. The cover of the 6 December 2004 issue of the New Yorker has an illustration by Carter Goodrich, in which Osama bin Laden hides in the crowds of New York as a grumpy, bell-ringing, sidewalk Santa. Hilarious.

So if we identify a red outfit, black belt, white beard, rosy cheeks and a hat, do we have Santa? Nope. That's a different Christmas season character: the Nutcracker. It's the hat, right? It can't just be any old hat...

But be careful!
That's a garden gnome.

Admittedly, there is a fine line between Santa and a garden gnome (mix in a few elves and you've got some suspicious genetic material, there), but what's clearly missing is the fur trim. It would appear that white fur trim is an essential characteristic of the Santa icon. In fact, it is the pointy red hat with fur trim that is donned by goofs and party goers throughout the Christmas season.

The diagram at right shows the basic progression from not-Santa to Santa:

... and from there to an infinite number of variations.

What can graphic designers learn from this? Anyone who has ever prepared a standards manual for a corporate identity is familiar with the concept of – if not the phrase – 'thou shalt not twist, twirl, stretch, squish,

FISHER PRICE HEAD

OLD MAN

GNOME

SANTA

rotate, extrude or animate the logo...' And anyone who has painstakingly prepared a logo 'lockup' with all the exact sizes, colours, fonts and spaces around logos that should or should not be used in any given instance, material or media also knows the frustration and sense of futility when each and every one of those rules are broken over time.

But what if the identity was built from the beginning to be so robust and so strong that it could withstand a huge amount of variation and still be recognizable as the company identity? What if it could eventually be Santa—ized (that is, changed, transformed, rendered in any medium, in whole or in part, abused and even mocked) to any person's whim or desire, and still maintain its essential nature as an icon of the company?

It has been done, but rarely. The most obvious contemporary case is Google, the logo that sports a different outfit every day. And yet still it is a readable word, and the fact that it is a word takes any of the guesswork out of the process. It would be much more interesting to have an icon with this kind of personality.

I would caution anyone that an icon that has worked its way over time into our hearts and minds would be more likely to survive such Santafication, but if you believe in the company you design for, if you believe they'll still be around a hundred years from now, I think this is a goal certainly worth aiming for. If you think of a logo in a new way, not as one that needs to be 'locked up' forever, but one that will eventually be set free... I believe if you think of Santa, well, incredible things might happen.

'Heaven is a place /
where nothing /
nothing ever happens.'

—Talking Heads, *Heaven*

T HE ONE THING WE ALL share, that we all know for a certainty, is that we are going to die. As well, at some point in our lives, we will know people who have died: people who are close to us, people who we will miss so much we have trouble continuing to live without them. It is common, and comforting, to think that they still exist in some form, that they perhaps are aware of us in our continuing lives and that we will see them again in some kind of afterlife.

Not being particularly versed in the specifics of common ideas of heaven, I had to do a little research on this subject – and I mean a little, because entire lives' studies could be (and surely are) devoted to parsing all the nuances, contradictions and interpretations of heaven in even

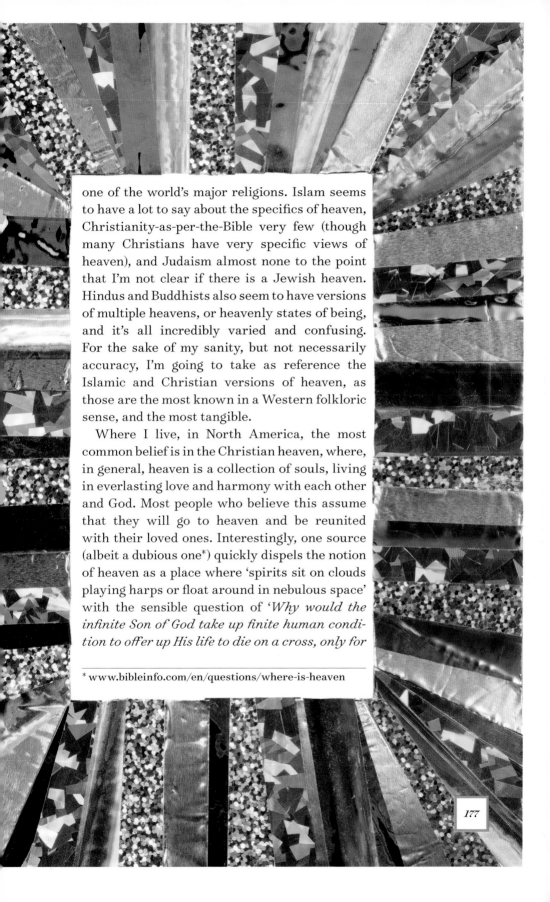

one of the world's major religions. Islam seems to have a lot to say about the specifics of heaven, Christianity-as-per-the-Bible very few (though many Christians have very specific views of heaven), and Judaism almost none to the point that I'm not clear if there is a Jewish heaven. Hindus and Buddhists also seem to have versions of multiple heavens, or heavenly states of being, and it's all incredibly varied and confusing. For the sake of my sanity, but not necessarily accuracy, I'm going to take as reference the Islamic and Christian versions of heaven, as those are the most known in a Western folkloric sense, and the most tangible.

Where I live, in North America, the most common belief is in the Christian heaven, where, in general, heaven is a collection of souls, living in everlasting love and harmony with each other and God. Most people who believe this assume that they will go to heaven and be reunited with their loved ones. Interestingly, one source (albeit a dubious one*) quickly dispels the notion of heaven as a place where 'spirits sit on clouds playing harps or float around in nebulous space' with the sensible question of *'Why would the infinite Son of God take up finite human condition to offer up His life to die on a cross, only for*

---

* www.bibleinfo.com/en/questions/where-is-heaven

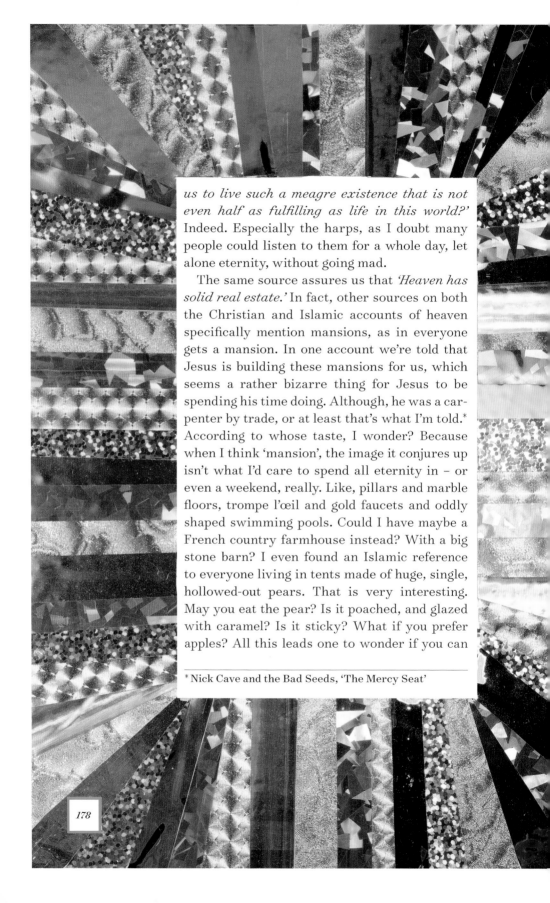

us to live such a meagre existence that is not even half as fulfilling as life in this world?' Indeed. Especially the harps, as I doubt many people could listen to them for a whole day, let alone eternity, without going mad.

The same source assures us that *'Heaven has solid real estate.'* In fact, other sources on both the Christian and Islamic accounts of heaven specifically mention mansions, as in everyone gets a mansion. In one account we're told that Jesus is building these mansions for us, which seems a rather bizarre thing for Jesus to be spending his time doing. Although, he was a carpenter by trade, or at least that's what I'm told.* According to whose taste, I wonder? Because when I think 'mansion', the image it conjures up isn't what I'd care to spend all eternity in – or even a weekend, really. Like, pillars and marble floors, trompe l'œil and gold faucets and oddly shaped swimming pools. Could I have maybe a French country farmhouse instead? With a big stone barn? I even found an Islamic reference to everyone living in tents made of huge, single, hollowed-out pears. That is very interesting. May you eat the pear? Is it poached, and glazed with caramel? Is it sticky? What if you prefer apples? All this leads one to wonder if you can

* Nick Cave and the Bad Seeds, 'The Mercy Seat'

order up what you want when you get there, or do you just have to take what you're given and be happy with it because happy is the only option in heaven?

In the Christian heaven only God sits on a throne, but some say that in the Islamic Paradise everyone gets a throne – a raised throne. What is the point of having a throne – the purpose of which is to lord it over everyone else that you're big and special and important – if everyone has one? Maybe just so you can see the other people in their raised thrones. Maybe it's like an SUV: you get one just so you can see at the same level as the other people in their SUVs/thrones, and you don't get stuck behind one with no view of what's going on (although there's nothing going on except people sitting in thrones – much like gridlocked traffic). And while, admittedly, I've never sat in a throne, they don't look that comfortable. All lumpy with diamonds and rubies set in cold, hard gold, maybe with a velvet cushion, at best. I think it would be better if everyone got an Arne Jacobsen Egg chair or an Eero Aarnio Ball chair. That seems way more heavenly to me.

Assuming that you get whatever you want (mansion, château, pear; throne, Egg chair, La-Z-Boy), are you stuck with it for all eternity? Like, the people in heaven who've been there for 2,000 years and got the very best gold throne

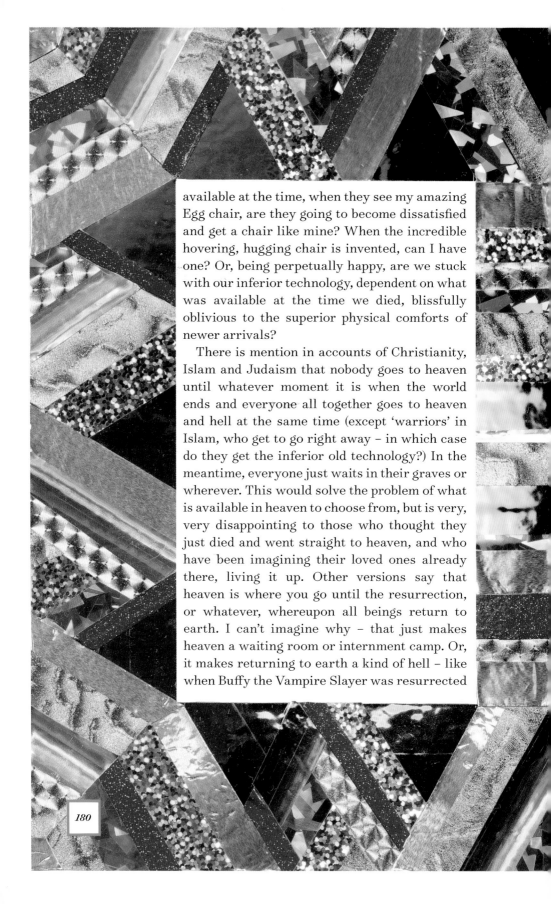

available at the time, when they see my amazing Egg chair, are they going to become dissatisfied and get a chair like mine? When the incredible hovering, hugging chair is invented, can I have one? Or, being perpetually happy, are we stuck with our inferior technology, dependent on what was available at the time we died, blissfully oblivious to the superior physical comforts of newer arrivals?

There is mention in accounts of Christianity, Islam and Judaism that nobody goes to heaven until whatever moment it is when the world ends and everyone all together goes to heaven and hell at the same time (except 'warriors' in Islam, who get to go right away – in which case do they get the inferior old technology?) In the meantime, everyone just waits in their graves or wherever. This would solve the problem of what is available in heaven to choose from, but is very, very disappointing to those who thought they just died and went straight to heaven, and who have been imagining their loved ones already there, living it up. Other versions say that heaven is where you go until the resurrection, or whatever, whereupon all beings return to earth. I can't imagine why – that just makes heaven a waiting room or internment camp. Or, it makes returning to earth a kind of hell – like when Buffy the Vampire Slayer was resurrected

and she was right pissed off about being called back to crappy earth after having a grand time swanning about in heaven.

In other versions of various religions there are different levels of heaven, where you might go when you die and then wait until the final, final, final judgment day and then maybe get into a higher heaven. Or, in Islam, there are multiple levels of heaven that you go to depending on your merits, with various perks and whatnot available to you depending on the level, kind of like the tiers of airline rewards programmes, which sounds like a recipe for dissatisfaction, if you ask me. In this model, you can talk to people in the other levels, but you can't go there or partake of their benefits, just as you can talk to your friend in Executive Class, but you may not share his fold-down bed, nor partake of his champagne and freshly baked chocolate chip cookies.

Are the people in heaven corporeal? Most accounts talk of being renewed, in that all your physical deformities are restored to perfection and you are in perfect health. This includes blindness, although I know for a fact that some people are perfectly happy being blind and would not welcome sudden sight. Islam is very clear that there is no homosexuality in heaven, so that 'perversion' is 'restored' to heterosexuality,

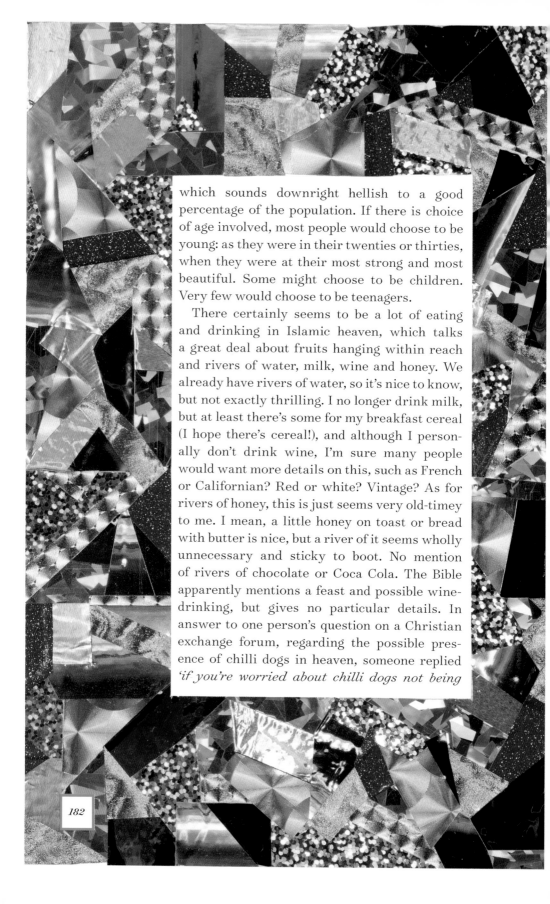

which sounds downright hellish to a good percentage of the population. If there is choice of age involved, most people would choose to be young: as they were in their twenties or thirties, when they were at their most strong and most beautiful. Some might choose to be children. Very few would choose to be teenagers.

There certainly seems to be a lot of eating and drinking in Islamic heaven, which talks a great deal about fruits hanging within reach and rivers of water, milk, wine and honey. We already have rivers of water, so it's nice to know, but not exactly thrilling. I no longer drink milk, but at least there's some for my breakfast cereal (I hope there's cereal!), and although I personally don't drink wine, I'm sure many people would want more details on this, such as French or Californian? Red or white? Vintage? As for rivers of honey, this is just seems very old-timey to me. I mean, a little honey on toast or bread with butter is nice, but a river of it seems wholly unnecessary and sticky to boot. No mention of rivers of chocolate or Coca Cola. The Bible apparently mentions a feast and possible wine-drinking, but gives no particular details. In answer to one person's question on a Christian exchange forum, regarding the possible presence of chilli dogs in heaven, someone replied *'if you're worried about chilli dogs not being*

in heaven, that's OK ... but I'm planning to be focused on praising the Father, the Son, and the Spirit, learning about Him, and having the totality of my being focused upon Him,' and then the thread was 'Closed as not constructive.' I think that pretty much answers that question from those particular Christians about their particular heaven: no chilli dogs and no fun.

So if there's eating and drinking, do we have internal organs? Do we get to experience a good bowel movement in heaven (surely one of life's great pleasures)? I somehow doubt it (no coprophiliacs in heaven – presumably another perversion that is purged once you get there). However, any fears of eternal constipation may be assuaged: Islam again rises to the occasion to address this by assuring us that eating results in no discomfort, and drinking wine results in no intoxication or hangover, and that food and drink are converted to beautiful smells. So that pretty much rules out internal organs that we know of, or any waste or repercussions from eating or drinking, however desirable those might be. I think maybe that guy asking about chilli dogs on the Christian forum should convert to Islam, as I have a feeling he's more likely to find heavenly satisfaction.

Much has been made of late regarding the 'seven virgins' that await Muslims in heaven.

Whether or not there are seven, there is certainly reference to beautiful young servants, male for the women and female virgins for the men. It's not clear to me that they are there to have sex with, but there is sex in Islamic heaven – but only between humans, not between humans and other beings such as angels or jinns (seemingly invisible beings made from smoke and fire; don't take my word for this). Men, predictably, get to have many wives – some say 70 to 100; women get to have one husband, i.e., it's Man-Heaven. Presumably there is sex. It's an odd place, where people who were married in life still see and talk to each other (probably from different levels of heaven), but also start over with new heavenly partners. What I really don't get is who or what are these beautiful eternal youths and virgins that serve them? They can't be human, or they would be in heaven with their own servants and virgins. Are they like robots? Or blow-up dolls? Can you talk to them? Are they good company? Or are they humans who are actually in their own personal hell, serving your every desire in your heaven? That sounds plausible.

I have always wondered what people actually do in heaven. People talk about communing with God, but ... then what? You can't just sit there, what would you talk about after, say, four hours, once you'd asked all the questions you wanted

to ask. Even if communing with God is just a feeling, it would still get pretty boring after a while. Some Christians say that Jesus is your friend, which is again, moderately interesting for a while, but not so much, as one presumably doesn't have any difference of opinion with him. The followers of Islam are pretty clearly living a version of life as we know it, eating and drinking things, sitting on thrones, looking at beautiful people, getting married. But how long can this go on? A few years? Decades? At some point you've simply got to become tired even of having your every wish fulfilled. Eternity is a really long time.

It seems most people really just want everlasting life, but there's nothing I can think of that I'd want to do forever. I once thought that heaven would be great if you could watch the world from any era, past or future, like TV, right down to whatever detail you wanted. This would be extremely cool ... for about 2–5 years. After that, I think the endless cycle of human drama would become extremely tiresome. Just as how there's only so many dog-playing-with-duck videos on the internet you can enjoy. The first few are delightful, but after that, yeah, seen it. Even meeting with my mother again, with all of our personality intact, I would very happily spend a week or more, just talking about

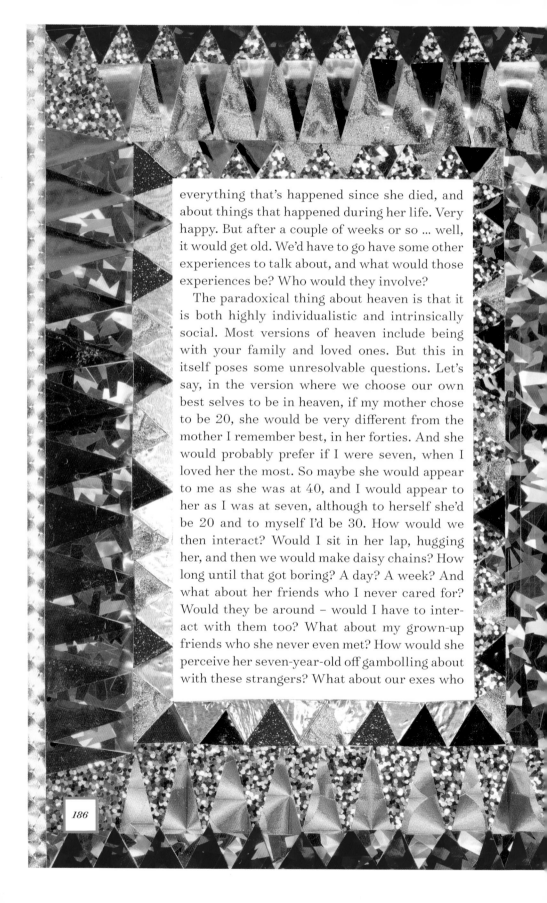

everything that's happened since she died, and about things that happened during her life. Very happy. But after a couple of weeks or so ... well, it would get old. We'd have to go have some other experiences to talk about, and what would those experiences be? Who would they involve?

The paradoxical thing about heaven is that it is both highly individualistic and intrinsically social. Most versions of heaven include being with your family and loved ones. But this in itself poses some unresolvable questions. Let's say, in the version where we choose our own best selves to be in heaven, if my mother chose to be 20, she would be very different from the mother I remember best, in her forties. And she would probably prefer if I were seven, when I loved her the most. So maybe she would appear to me as she was at 40, and I would appear to her as I was at seven, although to herself she'd be 20 and to myself I'd be 30. How would we then interact? Would I sit in her lap, hugging her, and then we would make daisy chains? How long until that got boring? A day? A week? And what about her friends who I never cared for? Would they be around – would I have to inter-act with them too? What about my grown-up friends who she never even met? How would she perceive her seven-year-old off gambolling about with these strangers? What about our exes who

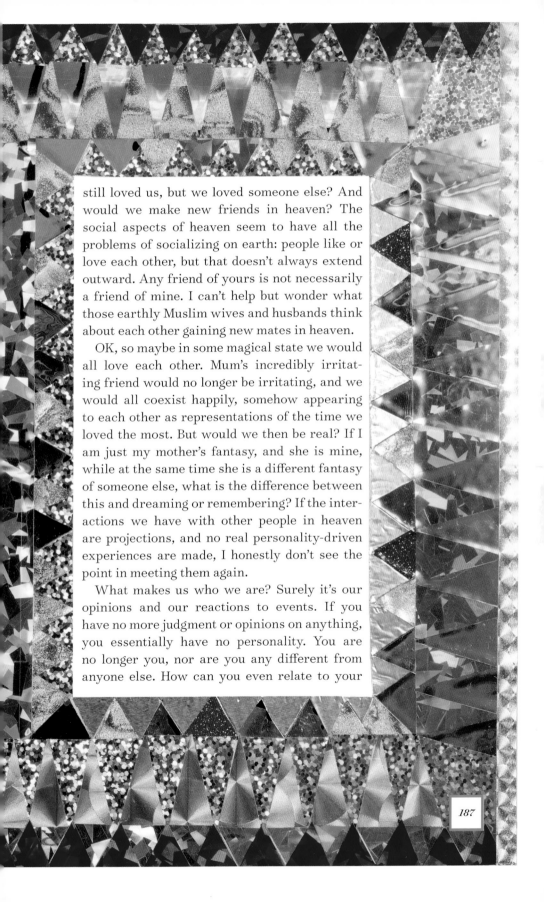

still loved us, but we loved someone else? And would we make new friends in heaven? The social aspects of heaven seem to have all the problems of socializing on earth: people like or love each other, but that doesn't always extend outward. Any friend of yours is not necessarily a friend of mine. I can't help but wonder what those earthly Muslim wives and husbands think about each other gaining new mates in heaven.

OK, so maybe in some magical state we would all love each other. Mum's incredibly irritating friend would no longer be irritating, and we would all coexist happily, somehow appearing to each other as representations of the time we loved the most. But would we then be real? If I am just my mother's fantasy, and she is mine, while at the same time she is a different fantasy of someone else, what is the difference between this and dreaming or remembering? If the interactions we have with other people in heaven are projections, and no real personality-driven experiences are made, I honestly don't see the point in meeting them again.

What makes us who we are? Surely it's our opinions and our reactions to events. If you have no more judgment or opinions on anything, you essentially have no personality. You are no longer you, nor are you any different from anyone else. How can you even relate to your loved ones in this? Being alive – really alive – is all about reacting to the things around in both positive and negative ways – to the differences in people: having conversations where you disagree, or where you agree on your disagreement with other people. Being human is placing value on things, liking some things more than others. So in heaven, if you're nothing like you were while alive, you're not even human. If we love everyone and everything, and happiness and acceptance are our only emotional states, what is the difference between us?

I suspect the proponents of spiritual heaven would say, 'Nothing. There is no longer any difference between us; we are one.' That may be, but it pretty much negates the idea of being reunited with your loved ones, and enjoying their company once again as we knew it on earth. And forget the mansions, thrones, food and drink and, really, any consciousness at all.

The biggest problem with the entire concept of heaven is that happiness is a relative state. You can only know happiness through knowing unhappiness, even if it's only to a small degree. So let's say you want to eat strawberries and whipped cream forever, you eat a lot of strawberries and you're happy, and you're happy, and you're happy, until eventually, you just don't want to eat them forever, so you're unhappy

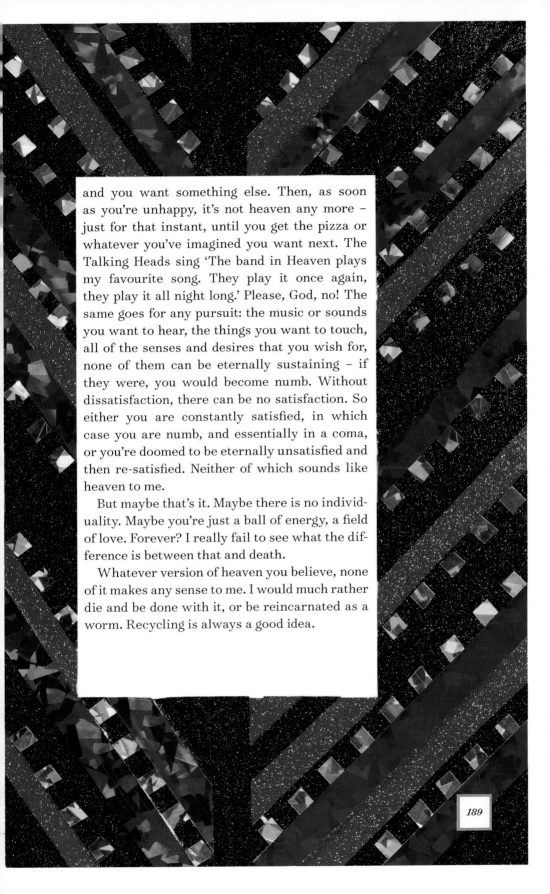

and you want something else. Then, as soon
as you're unhappy, it's not heaven any more –
just for that instant, until you get the pizza or
whatever you've imagined you want next. The
Talking Heads sing 'The band in Heaven plays
my favourite song. They play it once again,
they play it all night long.' Please, God, no! The
same goes for any pursuit: the music or sounds
you want to hear, the things you want to touch,
all of the senses and desires that you wish for,
none of them can be eternally sustaining – if
they were, you would become numb. Without
dissatisfaction, there can be no satisfaction. So
either you are constantly satisfied, in which
case you are numb, and essentially in a coma,
or you're doomed to be eternally unsatisfied and
then re-satisfied. Neither of which sounds like
heaven to me.

But maybe that's it. Maybe there is no individuality. Maybe you're just a ball of energy, a field
of love. Forever? I really fail to see what the difference is between that and death.

Whatever version of heaven you believe, none
of it makes any sense to me. I would much rather
die and be done with it, or be reincarnated as a
worm. Recycling is always a good idea.

THURS. March 7th

- phone LEFF for 16 lb. bag ✓
  EGRENODA (grey colour
  with purple edge)
- 7 pm CHARLIES (no pickerel, fresh)
- co of LETTUCE
- SCARF for ROD? They are smaller
  than I would like
- PINK TREE? the one is v. nice
- birthday present for Marion
  (look through sales at Sears)
- clean BOOT Need to be
- NEWSPAPERS Recycled Jane Urquhart
- could look for Stone Carver
  in Co-Op Library

- ask Anne B about Symphony
- ✓ FILM? So Monday only MONDAY
  POTATO 6:30 (phone Sunday to remind)
  AT HOME? left message
  phone Diana Sunday or tomorrow
  FRI, phone MICHAEL (& ROD)
  need GARLIC FRIDAY
  - Analesen & TRAEGERS
  - Lorelei boatmaster
  - NORA
  - JUDY & APPLES
  - Anne B. HAND CREAM

for what I learned in French and
Convassing judo
nod 819 7th ave N
      6:30 HURRY
Poli Sci X408
   should be back
nod $1.00 fine M.M.L.
      Mom phone   yes ☐
Angela Stern – 653-2051   no ☒

Mom - Call
Anne Coxworth

653-2403
May
I
Keep this.   It depends what for

Notes

MITTENS!!   make REQUE
JOB 3:30-4 pm & Quin Heckin
                652-3733
CRABMEAT (Sunday?)   CASH
✓ Parkis   Date no
  244-4224   H8 to 7   LETTE
  spray parsley
  phone Allyson at SES Mon morning
  (to go there??)
  one Mar 6 $19.08

FRI,   653-3892 Kalyna
  pork tenderloin?
✓ fish? Traeger
  phone Sharon Maku re il box
  cat claws? (or SAT)
  WATER PLANTS
  Megan left   phone
  343-7576   Anne
                  Stewart
  outside   say USS
  residence cat   sponsors
  Corridor 1st floor 653-343-
  poster etc for Mx
  TV   Desk downstairs USSU
  7 pm   get start
  Ch. 19 dental
          cafeteria
  TRACY table $7 + GST
         kiosk
  SAT,   down stairs Part 8 "Prison &
                     Alternatives"
  MILIE borrow
         Smichy   cheque
         from   IDEA Toronto
         classroom Box 500
         students   Toronto
         Lesy   M5W 1E6

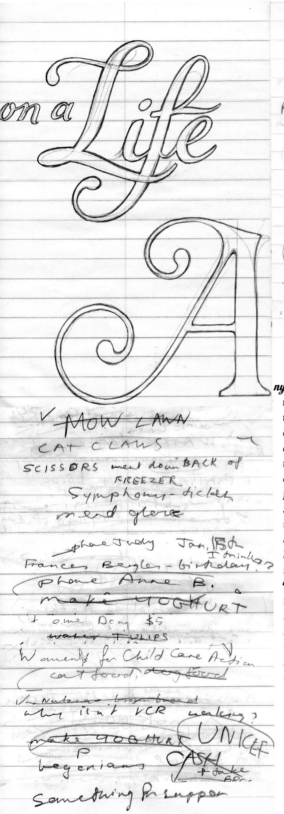

on a Life

Anyone who ever spent time at my mother's house may have noticed the upright steno notepad that she kept on the kitchen table or the counter. Ostensibly a *To Do* list, it also served as a notepad for things she heard on the radio, read in the paper, or thoughts and questions she had about sociology, anthropology, politics or any of her other interests. Since I was a kid, I can remember the anger I would invoke from her should I be so foolish as to remove one of the pages from a notebook: 'Those are my brains! You must NOT remove the pages!'

Her habit was to start on one side of the notebook, and when she reached the end, she turned it around and worked her way back through the reverse side of the pages until it was full. So to remove a page that had writing on the back was to remove a piece of her recorded memory. While I found this amusing, it wasn't until about three years before her death that I understood the significance of these notebooks, which we had come to refer to as Mum's Brains. That being, that they actually were. For it was this

unsuspected, low-tech medium that allowed her to keep functioning independently in her later years, masking the slow onset of aphasia and Alzheimer's without those of us close to her knowing. She had cheat sheets on her life.

When she died in December of 2006, we discovered a box of Brains, dated and archived, going back to 1972 (although, strangely, the 1980s were missing), and of all her possessions, this was the one I wanted the most. When I got them home I began going through them, and was surprised and delighted to see her life spring forth from the page.

In this increasingly digital age I have become especially fond of handwriting. My mother's is, of course, as familiar to me as my own, and here her handwriting danced and scrawled across the page. Important things were in all caps, sometimes with exclamation marks, circled, or all three. Tasks completed were checked off or crossed out, and some of the pages became crowded with additions and explanations forcing their

< This entry is strange, and I can only assume it had something to do with Mum's grandchildren.

< 1977
This surprised me! It makes a certain sense, given her politics, but it just doesn't seem like her kind of movie. It is, however, one of my favourites.

< No, she was not an early adopter of the electric car ... this is a common winter task in Saskatchewan, where it gets cold enough that cars have electric block heaters to keep the engine (and battery) from freezing.

make
YOGHURT

phone about chicken
WATER PLANTS [left
man, PICK PEAS?
SOAK
BEANS
phone re (10) Chicken

1973
Phone Judy Martin
Phone Karen Brander
2002 phone JUDY on Wednesday
2002 Phone Anne B or Karen SAT
FROST tonight
GILLIAN
BUTTERCRUNCH lettuce
TUES.
FINISH UP the phoning for
the Peace meeting
something for supper

CONGRATS – Mildred Ken
some vacuuming
Barbara owes me $9.70

CAT CLAWS
play dough 10 tsp

John Ralston Saul – Voltaire's
Bastards?
or his latest? (Massey
Unconscious Civilization
and
WRAP PARCELS

!! URGENT !!

LIBRARY BOOKS
Tues. Savoy Cabbage
Phone Pat Adams
2001 phi Pat Adams re Thurs.
cttee mtg.
EAVESTROUGHS

TITLES CHEESE!
what to do with asparagus?
Wash garage door

A small
Savoy
cabbage
try bread
at Rolo's?

2 tbs
oil

This involved >
making Play-Doh, not
buying it.

1976 >
This was a message
to me: wrapping
presents was one of
my jobs.

1972

way into the page, or roped off with squiggly lines. Expressive, imperative, personal.

I never could define my mother's sense of humour, although we always laughed together. Whatever it was still comes through in these seemingly mundane lists. Her questions and commands to herself, and the quirky urgency of such entries as '**CHEESE!**' strike me as inexplicably funny.

A diary records the things we think are worth recording, either to ourselves or to the imagined 'other' reading our fantasy biography. A diary is highly selective in what it records, and/or is intensely personal, as a cathartic space for angst and ecstasy. But what I realized with Mum's Brains was that what I held was both so much less and so much more. It was an actual, day-to-day account of the minutiae that makes up a life; all the mundane detail that gets lost in the vortex of our everyday existence. If ever you have wondered how on earth you spend your time, well, here it is.

DON'T BOTHER ME WHEN I'M ON THE PHONE

Marian or Rod

Please remove
dead mouse
from hall

Thanks
Mum

Melanie wants me to go to
a movie at 1:00
What movie? about a guy who twins will rule and when they grow up they do something for him in return
Can you pay for it? I need months pocket money
We will see to
vacuuming tomorrow
or take $1 & give me a receipt M.B.

Dr. Warner Phoned

ROD
your muffler is full
of holes
Thursday

Marian
Dust before watching
more TV

Make list pros & cons
of school camp
What?

MONSTER

I might not be
back until after six.
I have a long exam.

In this, it's paradoxically universal and idiosyncratic. We all attend to household chores, buy groceries, pay bills and keep in contact with friends, but there is something about the specific things my mother did and bought, and how she wrote messages to herself that conjure up a surprisingly coherent image of her life and personality. We see ourselves as actors in some grand opera of life, but we exist behind the scenes, in eternal preparation. All of these moments are usually lost, both in official record and in our memory, but here they are, preserved.

The notebooks from the early '70s are like a window into our family. Both of my brothers were still living at home, and the notebooks contain messages from each of us to the other, and the occasional back-and-forth conversation, some of them in real time. This is what distance communication was like before cell phones and texting. As each of us came and went from the house we added to the notes: where we were; when we'd be back; ques-

< 1976
This was from my brother, Rod, to me. In this case, 'Monster' was used affectionately. I think.

194

POTATO
7 p.m.

When O've finished
talking O'll talk to you

But I need your
help!!!! Please Hurry!!!!

WAIT,
HURRY!!

Marian   work

owe ~~20~~ mins from Thurs, 5th
~~30 mins from Fri, 6th~~
~~70 mins from Mon 9th~~

done ✓   30 mins Tues. 10th
~~30~~ 35 mins. from 11th

652-0500   30   12th

~~70~~ left
~~55~~

MARIAN

I will be home
LATE (class till 5.30 +)

please TURN ON
OVEN to 400°F

at 5 p.m

I will be very very
cross if I come home &
find no baked potato
for me

6.10 potato.

tions, requests and answers. My mother worked and attended university, so there are frequent requests from her to my brothers to prepare meals or otherwise take up the chores of a caregiver for me, the youngest. Even I am kept to a schedule of tasks and 'time owed' for housework, in lists that appear with hours and minutes tabulated and amended, in an ongoing time 'bank'. **There is** also a lot of monetary banking that goes on, as family petty cash is recorded going out, for what purpose, and change owed. What surprised and amused me was that the lending and borrowing of small amounts of money to and from friends and family continued throughout Mum's life. It was as though she were operating a microfinance bank, with each transaction recorded to the cent. Almost comically small

MOOT
I AM AT
THE MENDE
WITH
MICKEY
MOUSE

1979>>
At far right is a note from me. 'Moot' was short for Mutti; 'Mickey Mouse' = my brother, Mike.

195

and precise amounts of owed cash are frequently noted. Indeed, it reminded me of my mother's insistence on repaying me for groceries in exact change when I visited as an adult – despite my protests. I would try to wave it off, but she diligently counted it out to the nickel and penny, or, if she didn't have the change, might say, 'I still owe you 25 cents' (and write it down).

Much of this is a result of our family existing below the poverty level, particularly prior to the mid-1970s. My mother never took money for granted, and perhaps because of this, or perhaps because of a different sensibility and time, I have noticed in her notebooks a record of a distinct lack of waste. She mended things, used the library almost daily, made a lot of food from scratch, used up food that was about to go bad, and recycled materials long before it was common or environmentally conscionable.

My mother was politically left wing, a strong feminist, and very active in her

< 1996
My mother began to struggle with new technology. She never did figure out email, and for years would write notes for my brother Michael to send to her half-sister Barbara in the UK.

< She loved camping.

< 1995
Given that she made a perfectly good regular shepherd's pie, it distresses me to see this entry, long after the dreaded '70s food fads.

< 1977

< 2001

196

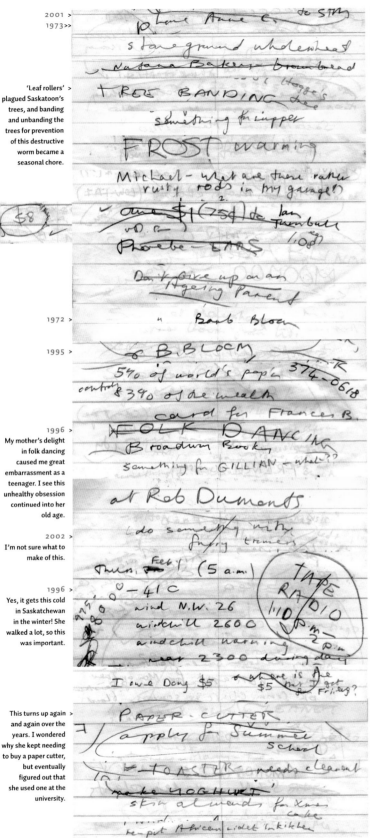

'Leaf rollers'
plagued Saskatoon's
trees, and banding
and unbanding the
trees for prevention
of this destructive
worm became a
seasonal chore.

1972 >

1995 >

1996 >
My mother's delight
in folk dancing
caused me great
embarrassment as a
teenager. I see this
unhealthy obsession
continued into her
old age.

2002 >
I'm not sure what to
make of this.

1996 >
Yes, it gets this cold
in Saskatchewan
in the winter! She
walked a lot, so this
was important.

This turns up again >
and again over the
years. I wondered
why she kept needing
to buy a paper cutter,
but eventually
figured out that
she used one at the
university.

politics and beliefs. She
believed in social change
through grass-roots action,
and her activity in support
of a variety of causes
throughout the 1970s is
simply mind-boggling. Her
daunting schedule of
meetings, picketings and
canvassing was kept
elsewhere, and surprisingly
only creeps into these
notebooks when changes of
dates or times are noted; my
favourite being a message
from my brother that
announces, **Picketing is off
tonight. Tell everyone.** But her
politics are evident in the
books she notes, and in the
random jottings she has
clearly made while listening
to the radio: questions,
exclamations and statistics
attest to her interests and
political ideology.

A great deal of the notebooks
are devoted to food, and I
regained a familiarity with
my mothers tastes – often
evoking the brown rice
culinary style of the '70s
radical. She grew sprouts,
soaked beans and made her
own granola and yoghurt
– the yoghurt-making at
least continued to 2002.
She was specific about
bread: **crusty brown buns,**

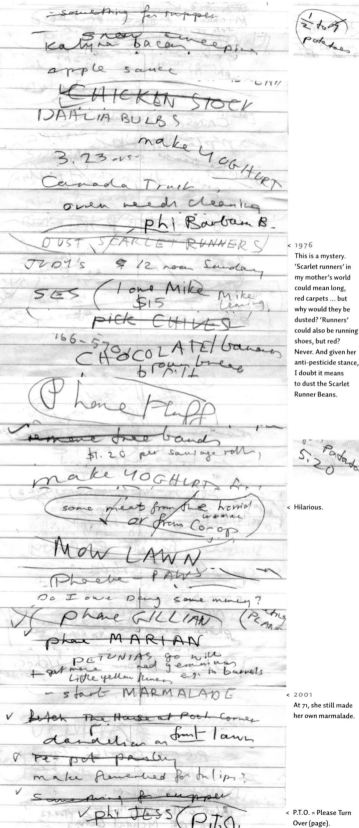

Nutana whole wheat, Traeger's rye bread. Cheese, BUTTER, honey and chocolate appear frequently, causing me to wonder why she was never fat. Some of the entries are amusing, such as PICKEREL??? Should she? Should she buy pickerel? And there are frequent notes about free-range chickens – where, when, how big, how much, how many – which over the course of a couple of weeks devolve into increasingly cryptic and funny remarks: 10 not 8 Chickens, Phone re: Chickens, get Chickens, Chickens and, eventually, CHICKENS!!!

Use Bacon sounds like something from the Pork Authority Board, but attests to her diligence in not wasting food. The specific and exotic sounding Small Savoy Cabbage turns up, only to reappear, ominously, several pages later as Use Savoy Cabbage.

Still, there are mysteries. The lists do not contain any items such as detergents, toothpaste, soap or toilet paper. Nor does it include some common grocery items

< 1976
This is a mystery. 'Scarlet runners' in my mother's world could mean long, red carpets … but why would they be dusted? 'Runners' could also be running shoes, but red? Never. And given her anti-pesticide stance, I doubt it means to dust the Scarlet Runner Beans.

< Hilarious.

< 2001
At 71, she still made her own marmalade.

< P.T.O. = Please Turn Over (page).

1972

2000 >

1996

2002

1976

1996

2001

2002

claws clipped

Pub. Lib.

Taming of the Shrew

As You Like It

ANNE SMART

dog whistle?

use LEEKS o zucchini

Rye bread / sourdough

phone re CHICKENS

BBC "Much Ado" shd be here Monday

Branagh "Much Ado"

phi JUDY

lettuce / sprouts

where is nightlight?? 3p.m.

Regeneration

POTATO ¼ to 7

wash basement window

chocolate

MACKEREL on Thursday

Peter Prebble

Peter Prebble 653-7331

CARD for Peter Prebble OUT

textbook for Georgie T.

Elisabeth

MON 9:30 TV Ch. 12

MILK, bananas more BUTTER

POTATOS PHOEBE

phi Marian / Dante re time & no. of flight on Thu.

- juice and cereal - which I know my mother ate regularly. There must have been another grocery list that she took to the store. But why milk and butter, but not cereal? These are things I will never know. **The notebooks** also served as a timer for food like eggs and potatoes, where most of the pages have scribbled references to the time something went into the oven, attesting to the frequency with which she referred to the notebook. **My brother**, Rod, has described my mother as a 'kin-keeper', because she filled the role of one who kept people together and in touch, both with her family and friends. Certainly the amount of phoning she did is astonishing, and as I read through the notebooks I see frequent references to the names of all her friends as they recur day after day over the years. Along with a litany of unfamiliar names, I see all of her good friends of 30 years or more: **Judy, Marjorie, Barbara, Anne(s), Karen, Franziska, Terry, Rob, Joanna, Peter** ... I am certain that every person who significantly passed through my mum's life is mentioned in these pages. Some of those who appear in the 1972 notebooks are still there in 2002 as she continued her reminders to keep in touch, give birthday presents, recommend books and host or attend dinners.

I and my two brothers, Michael and Rod, appear on most of the pages, even after we left home, as she called us every week. Our father, Dennis, divorced from Mum since 1965, also appears with consistent regularity, as they remained friends throughout her life. *There are* also frequent references to her pets. There is something about the words **CAT CLAWS** that I find compelling, and **CHEW STICKS** has that familiar commanding tone. References to her dog, Dounia, are replaced eventually by reminders regarding Phoebe – a truly dreadful beast whom I thought of as the 'Hound of the Baskervilles'. She loved that dog, and much to my amazement, there is a 1996 note that practices a classified ad to give her away. This would have been around the time that she was having trouble between Phoebe and her new grandchildren (telling in the line of the ad, **not best with young children**), and I can only imagine how hard it must have been for her to even contemplate placing it. In the end, she didn't, or maybe she did and there were no takers, because Phoebe stayed with her to her end.

When Phoebe died I thought my mother's pet tyranny was over, but Phoebe was immediately succeeded by Sukey the cat, who quickly took control as ruler of the household. While the last of Mum's notebooks have disappeared, I can remember seeing them on her table recording ever-smaller minutiae, with reminders to turn off the kettle, check the stove, and endless notes of **Sukey is OUT, Sukey is IN, Sukey is OUT, Sukey is IN**, ad nauseum, as though Sukey were a very important person and Mum her secretary ... which, of course, she was.

All of these insignificancies, taken together, form a kind of a pattern. A rhythm of time and experience emerges. I can watch the seasons pass, as there are reminders to buy geraniums, impatiens and lilies of the valley, to weed the garden, mow the lawn, pick gooseberries and rake leaves, followed by frost warnings and reminders to plug in the car and shovel snow.

Food, friends, family, pets, directions, TV shows to watch, notes from the radio, problems with her car, book titles, appointments, meetings, bills to pay, oven times, questions, answers … the repetition of chores and people and food weave a kind of fabric of life. Her life, my life, all our lives are somehow reflected in these pages. These are the things we do every day that make us both the unique people we are and members of something bigger and more universal than our own tiny lives.

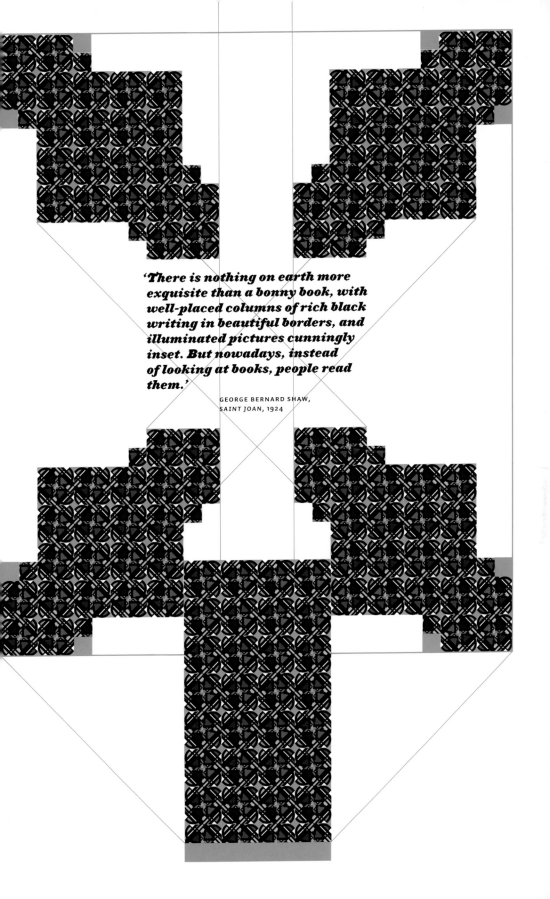

'*There is nothing on earth more exquisite than a bonny book, with well-placed columns of rich black writing in beautiful borders, and illuminated pictures cunningly inset. But nowadays, instead of looking at books, people read them.*'

GEORGE BERNARD SHAW,
SAINT JOAN, 1924

SOURCES

Alexander, J. J. G., *Medieval Illuminators and Their Methods of Work* (New Haven, Connecticut and London: Yale University Press, 1994).

Berger, John, *About Looking* (London: Bloomsbury, 2009).

———, *Ways of Seeing* (London: British Broadcasting Corporation, 1972).

Bocskay, Georg, et al., *Mira Calligraphiae Monumenta: A Sixteenth-Century Calligraphic Manuscript* (Malibu, California: J. Paul Getty Museum, 1992).

Brown, Michelle, *Manuscripts from the Anglo-Saxon Age* (Toronto: University of Toronto Press, 2007).

Clemens, Raymond, and Timothy Graham, *Introduction to Manuscript Studies* (Ithaca, New York: Cornell University Press, 2007).

Coffin, Sarah, *Rococo: The Continuing Curve, 1730–2008* (New York: Cooper-Hewitt National Design Museum, 2008).

Daston, Lorraine, and Katharine Park, *Wonders and the Order of Nature, 1150–1750* (New York: Zone Books, 1998).

De Hamel, Christopher, *A History of Illuminated Manuscripts* (London: Phaidon Press, 2006).

———, *The British Library Guide to Manuscript Illumination: History and Techniques* (Toronto: University of Toronto Press, 2001).

Gombrich, E. H., *Art and Illusion: A Study in the Psychology of Pictorial Representation* (London: Phaidon, 1960).

———, *The Sense of Order: A Study in the Psychology of Decorative Art* (London: Phaidon, 1979; 1984).

———, *The Story of Art* (London: Phaidon, 1950; 2006).

Grabar, Oleg, *Masterpieces of Islamic Art: The Decorated Page from the 8th to the 17th Century* (Munich: Prestel, 2009).

Gruber, Christiane J., *The Islamic Manuscript Tradition: Ten Centuries of Book Arts in Indiana University Collections* (Bloomington, Indiana: Indiana University Press, 2010).

Helfand, Jessica, *Scrapbooks: An American History* (New Haven, Connecticut and London: Yale University Press, 2008).

Jackson, Deirdre Elizabeth, *Marvellous to Behold: Miracles in Medieval Manuscripts* (London: British Library, 2007).

Jones, Owen, *The Grammar of Ornament* (1856; London: Studio Editions, 1986).

Khatibi, Abdelkebir, and Mohamed Sijelmassi, *The Splendour of Islamic Calligraphy* (London: Thames & Hudson, 1996).

Knowles, Elizabeth, *The Oxford Dictionary of Quotations* (Oxford: Oxford University Press, 1999).

Lings, Martin, *Splendours of Qur'an Calligraphy and Illumination* (Liechtenstein: Thesaurus Islamicus Foundation, 2005).

———, *Symbol and Archetype: A Study of the Meaning of Existence* (Louisville, Kentucky: Fons Vitae, 2005).

Loos, Adolf, 'Ornament and Crime' (Innsbruck: 1908; trans. into English, 1913).

Luthi, Ann Louise, *Sentimental Jewellery* (Princes Risborough, Buckinghamshire: Shire Publications, 2001).

Morris, William, 'The Lesser Arts', in *Hopes and Fears for Art* (London: Ellis & White, 1882; originally a lecture titled 'The Decorative Arts: Their Relation to Modern Life and Progress', given in 1877).

——, *Art and the Beauty of the Earth* (London: Longmans & Co., 1899; originally a lecture of the same title, given in 1881).

Naylor, Gillian, *William Morris by Himself: Designs and Writings* (Boston: Little, Brown and Co, 1996).

Palgrave, Sir Francis, 'The Fine Arts in Florence', in *Quarterly Review* LXVI (September 1840): 313–54.

Pevesner, Nikolaus, *Pioneers of Modern Design: From William Morris to Walter Gropius* (New York: Museum of Modern Art, 1949; originally published as *Pioneers of the Modern Movement*, by Faber & Faber, London, 1936).

Piotrovsky, Mikhail, and John Vrieze, *Earthly Beauty, Heavenly Art: The Art of Islam* (Amsterdam: De Nieuwe Kerk, 1999).

Postrel, Virginia I., *The Substance of Style: How the Rise of Aesthetic Value is Remaking Commerce, Culture, and Consciousness* (New York: HarperCollins, 2003).

Pugin, A. W. N., *The True Principles of Pointed or Christian Architecture* (London: John Weale, 1841).

Racinet, Auguste, M. Dupont-Auberville and David Batterham, *The World of Ornament* (Cologne: Taschen, 2006).

Rhie, Marylin M., and Robert A. F. Thurman, *Worlds of Transformation: Tibetan Art of Wisdom and Compassion* (New York: Tibet House, 1999).

Ruskin, John, *The Seven Lamps of Architecture* (London: Smith, Elder & Co., 1849).

——, *The Stones of Venice* (London: Smith, Elder & Co., 1851–53).

Santayana, George, *The Sense of Beauty: Being the Outline of Aesthetic Theory* (New York: Dover Publications, 1985).

Shaw, George Bernard, *Saint Joan* (London: Constable & Co., 1924).

Sims, Eleanor, B. I. Marshak, and Ernst J. Grube, *Peerless Images: Persian Painting and Its Sources* (New Haven, Connecticut and London: Yale University Press, 2002).

Trilling, James, *Ornament: A Modern Perspective* (Seattle: University of Washington Press, 2003).

——, *The Language of Ornament* (London: Thames & Hudson, 2001).

Warde, Beatrice, 'The Crystal Goblet, or Printing Should Be Invisible' (1932), in *The Crystal Goblet: Sixteen Essays on Typography* (Cleveland and New York: World Publishing, 1956).

Wilde, Oscar, 'The Critic as Artist', in *Intentions* (London: James R. Osgood, McIlvaine & Co, 1891).

Woodcock, Thomas, and John Martin Robinson, *The Oxford Guide to Heraldry* (Oxford: Oxford University Press, 1988).

NOTES ON THE PRODUCTION

All artwork and design, unless otherwise noted, is original work by Marian Bantjes. *Throughout:* most of the folios are set in **HFJ Acropolis Black Italic** (by Hoefler & Co.), except where noted.

Cover
    ART: All of the artwork on the front cover is created in Illustrator with custom type.
    FONT: (back cover) **HFJ Acropolis Black Italic** (by Hoefler & Co.).

Half-title
    ART: Vector art, patterning tiles.
    FONT: FF SERIA ITALIC CAPITALS (by Martin Majoor).

Title
    ART: Vector art, patterning tiles and custom type.

Dedication
    ART: Vector art, patterning tiles.
    FONT: Huronia (by Ross Mills, Tiro Typeworks).

Copyright
    ART: Vector art, patterning tiles.
    FONT: A2 Typewriter (designed by and generously on loan from Henrik Kubel, A2/SW/HK), with Auto 2 (by Underware).

Contents
    ART: Vector art, patterning tiles.
    FONT: Huronia and FF SERIA ITALIC CAPITALS.

Acknowledgments pages x–xiii
    ART: Custom type in vector art.
    FONT: *Huronia Italic.*

Foreword pages xiv–xvi
    ART: The lettering and ornaments were created out of cereal (Shredded Wheat and granola, if you must know) and arranged in Photoshop.
    FONT: Huronia.

Quotations pages 1, 139, 187
    FONTS: **HFJ Acropolis Black Italic** with Auto 2.

Introduction pages 2–9
    ART: The art for this was inspired by the decorations and offerings to deities in Bali that are set out on the street every evening. Some of these were made in Bali using local flowers, stems, leaves and palm fronds, which I either bought in the market or harvested from the garden where I was staying. The rest were made at my home, with leaves and flowers from my own garden. Various arrangements were assembled and stitched together with grasses and fern stems, then photographed and arranged in repetitions in Photoshop.
The titling and initial capital W I made out of larger flower petals.
    FONTS: Huronia and **FF Seria Bold Italic.**